PEWTER
of the Channel Isla[nds]

The flagons and measures of th[e Channel] Islands hold an exceptional posi[tion in the] history and development of Europea[n pewter] which for all practical purposes is sy[nonymous] with World pewter. These tiny British Islands of Jersey, Guernsey, Alderney and Sark, lying just off the French coast, are, quite re- markably, identified with two distinctive patterns of flagons and measures, dating from the beginning of the XVIIIth century or earlier and which are not found anywhere else in the world. Still more extraordinary, a large per- centage of these vessels were made, not in the Islands themselves, but in England, apparently solely for export to the Islands. They were, moreover, produced in considerable quantities and, relative to the size of the Islands, a sub- stantial number are still extant.

The origins of these pieces, who made them, when and where make a fascinating story set against a background of the history, social life and customs of these Islands with their unique relationship to Britain and the English Crown, but with close cultural and trading links with France. This work not only deals fully with these subjects but also examines in detail the physical characteritsics of the different types of flagons and measures and, supported by detailed statistics of a large number of pieces examined, explains how to distinguish and date them.

This is the first comprehensive work dealing with the Pewter of The Channel Islands and, although some questions still remain to be answered, it will provide the reader, be he expert or tyro, with a fund of information which will enable him to start collecting in this field with confidence, or, if he has already commenced, to add considerably to his know- ledge of and interest in the subject. For those who do not collect Channel Islands pewter, or even perhaps any pewter at all, this work should still make absorbing reading dealing as it does with familiar, essential objects in daily use in the home, the church and the pub and closely connected with the social life of the inhabitants of these interesting Islands from the beginning of the XVIIIth century or earlier.

ENGLAND

London

Isle of Wight

Cherbourg

NORMANDY

*Falaise

Granville

*Avranches

FRANCE

Pewter of the Channel Islands

PEWTER
of the
Channel Islands

by

Stanley C. Woolmer, FRIBA, FRTPI

Member of the Pewter Society
Member of the Pewter Collectors Club of America
in association with

Charles H. Arkwright
Corresponding Member of The Pewter Society

FRONTISPIECE Jersey and Guernsey quart
flagons with Jersey and Guernsey 'lilies'
Amaryllis Belladonna and *Nerine Sarniensis.*
(Photo: C. Arkwright).

John Bartholomew
Edinburgh

Universitas
BIBLIOTHECA
Ottaviensis

Front end papers: Map showing the
Channel Islands in relation to England
and France.
(C. Arkwright and R. Paton).

312464

© Stanley C. Woolmer,
and Charles H. Arkwright
First published 1973
by John Bartholomew and Son Ltd.
12 Duncan Street, Edinburgh EH9 1TA
Also at 216 High Street, Bromley BR1 1PW

ISBN 0 85152 933-X

Designed by Youé and Spooner Ltd.

Filmset by Keyspools Ltd, Golborne Lancashire
Printed in Great Britain
by Butler & Tanner Ltd, Frome, Somerset
ISBN 0 85152 933-X

NK
8415
.G7W66
1973

Table of Contents

Introduction

There are three maxims which the author of any new book needs to observe, the first that he should know exactly what he wants to say; the second that he should know how to present his subject, and the third, and perhaps the most important, to know when to stop. All of these are adequately covered in the present work. I have known of Stanley Woolmer's interest in this particular field of study for many years, and, like him, have bemoaned the fact that no one has ever attempted, in print, seriously to classify the various types of pewter measures and flagons which have been in use in the Channel Islands from time immemorial.

Many collectors of antique pewterware have been aware only that certain forms of vessels were indigenous to the *Iles Anglo-Normandes*, and the more observant might, perhaps, have noted that no exactly similar types existed elsewhere. Despite what, at the outset, seemed a limited field of research, it is the more surprising that no serious studies had been undertaken even into the capacities of the various styles, and it had been assumed that, originally, ancient French, and, later, modern metric standards had been adopted, and that, later still, British Imperial measures had prevailed, and here collectors seem to have been content to leave the matter. Intensive studies have shown that the Islands have each known and used their own individual standards to the exclusion of outside influences, and that it is only in the present century that they have been persuaded to conform to a common standard. About all that was known for certain was that some forms of measures could be located to one or the other of the two main islands, Jersey or Guernsey, by certain very definite characteristics, but beyond this no serious attempts had been made to categorise the intermediate types which did not fit into any hard and fast grouping.

I am honoured to have been asked to write an introduction to this study, into which I know has gone so much thought and tireless effort, and I am positive that none of those involved in the project ever realised where it was likely to lead. From the outset I have been aware of the co-authors' intentions to produce something useful in print as a guide to any interested party who needed to have a handy source of reference in one volume of facts which, in many cases, were not readily available even to residents in the Channel Islands themselves.

Collectors, students, historians, and many others, on both sides of the Channel, and, of course, in the Islands themselves, will find much here to intrigue them, and all should be grateful to the authors for their careful—indeed, meticulous—presentation of all the presently available facts.

The co-authors were jointly and individually suited to undertake the study which has culminated in this most worthwhile and readable book; each has contributed his own particular talent or interest to the whole, and there is no doubt that the final published work will take its place as a 'standard' for many years to come: yet they, perhaps more than anyone else, will realise that, although what they have produced is as complete as it can be *at time of going to press* it will, nevertheless, always be incomplete, as must be any pioneering effort, but it will, they hope, inspire others who have access to hitherto unpublished data, or to little known examples of Channel Islands pewterware, to compare their own findings with what has been produced herein, with a view to promoting still further both interest and knowledge for posterity.

Ronald F. Michaelis
Newhaven, Sussex
October 1972

Preface

The collector of English or continental pewter can, in time, hope to acquire examples of almost every kind of domestic utensil as well as of tavern measures, tankards and ecclesiastical articles such as patens and chalices. For the collector of Channel Islands pewter however, there are only Jersey and Guernsey lidded flagons, which are quite distinct one from the other, and Jersey unlidded measures. Typical examples of the Jersey and Guernsey lidded types appear in Plate I and of the unlidded measures in Plates xv, LXII, LXIII and LXIV. These are the only pieces—of clearly defined forms—which have been specifically designated as Channel Islands pewter during the 70 years or so since pewter became of interest as a collector's item and the first books were written about collecting it. In this book, however, we have also noted plates and porringers used in the Islands and made both by the makers of Channel Islands flagons and measures and by other pewterers who were of Channel Islands origin.

The Channel Islands—'as every schoolboy knows'—consist of Jersey, Guernsey, Alderney and Sark (and several other smaller islands). They are some 100 miles from the nearest point of England but only 15 miles from the coast of France, a fact which has had considerable influence on the history, customs and life of these Islands and their inhabitants.

Although Sovereignty over the Islands has resided in the British Crown since 1066 they are not part of the United Kingdom and are self-governing for all internal purposes. Moreover, they are not administered as a single unit. Jersey has its own States or Parliament as has Guernsey: Sark, while part of the 'Bailiwick of Guernsey', has its own 'Chief Pleas': Alderney is now in a similar position to Sark but before the 1939 War, was independent.

It is quite extraordinary that these small islands, with a total area of only 75 square miles, have been identified with two quite distinct patterns of flagons and measures not found anywhere else in the world. It is a measure of the individuality which their inhabitants have maintained in so many spheres of life throughout their history. Moreover each Island has clung tenaciously to its own pattern—even today almost all the flagons found in Jersey are of the Jersey pattern, and similarly it is the Guernsey pattern that is primarily found in that Island. As far as Sark is concerned it seems that, at least from the 18th century onwards, primarily Guernsey type flagons were used in the Island and we have been told by Dame Sybil Hathaway, the present Dame, that, dating from Tudor times when the Island was colonised from Jersey, every holder of a 'Ténement' or farm was obliged by law to have in his possession an approved pewter measure for the dispensing of milk, cider, etc. Alderney had pewter vessels in its Church until 1939, but they all disappeared during the German occupation and that Island therefore does not figure in this work.

Pewterware was almost certainly in use in the Islands as early as anywhere else in Europe, but, so far, we have found mention of it only in laws, inventories and other documents dating from the late sixteenth century. As far as extant pewter is concerned, the earliest dating about which we can feel certain is around 1700, but pewterware could have been made in the Islands, or at least in Jersey, well before that date. The basis for this statement is that we know, from several reliable sources, that regular, small, legal shipments of tin were made to the Islands from Cornwall from the second half of the seventeenth century. Before that time, as well as afterwards, there was a lively trade in smuggled tin, i.e. 'uncoined' tin, which had not suffered the proper tax at origin.

The Islands had an old and long lasting expertise in smuggling: their sea captains used to sail to the Newfoundland Banks, pick up a cargo of cod and then sail on to Boston to barter cod for tobacco. Thence they sailed to Lisbon or perhaps to a Spanish port or, if there was no war with France, to a French port, there bartering fish for wine or brandy. Their cargo entered Guernsey duty-free and was picked up by Cornish smugglers ('Brandy for the parson, baccy for the clerk'): the quid pro quo was tin brought from Cornwall to the Islands. Jean Chevalier, a local official, recorded in his Diary, 1643–1651, several shipments, some smuggled, which reached Jersey and found a ready market in the Island, though it is not clear whether the tin was bought for local use or for re-export. Some of the smugglers, driven into Jersey by bad weather, carried cargoes of tin destined for France. One who sought shelter in Jersey had buried the ingots in a cargo of horse manure. Surely a rather naïve faith in the gullibility of any English preventive officer who might have boarded his ship!

We make no apology for our inability to state categorically where certain of the makers of Channel Islands pewter worked, or, indeed, who they were. Although the Islands are rich in manuscript archives, the shortage of qualified archivists or historians in such small communities is such that it may take decades to sort and codify these records. It is a matter for gratitude that so much has already been done. There are no printed broadsheets which might have helped and no newspapers before the last fifteen years of the eighteenth century and, even then, hardly any advertisements mentioning pewter and none at all containing references to pewterers. Inscribed pieces are as rare as black swans. As a result, our conclusions are based, in the main, firstly, on the stylistic variations within each group and on the maker's mark, if any, and secondly, on such records as registers of baptisms, marriages and burials. Unfortunately, Jersey burial registers generally give no information as to the parentage or age of the deceased, much less his erstwhile profession. As a result, in the chapter devoted to the individual makers, we have been able only to indicate the degree of our faith in our conclusions ranging from firm conviction to purely conjectural! The reader is at liberty to agree or disagree. As knowledge increases, collectors will, we hope, be able to promote or demote the strength of our beliefs.

We have, however, been able to show conclusively that Channel Islands pewter, even extant pewter, is much earlier than it has been thought to be by previous writers on British pewter who have touched on Channel Islands wares en passant.

It is hoped that the detailed analyses of Island

flagons given in the later chapters of this book, and in the Appendices, will help collectors to discriminate between the various flagons in their collections and to date them. There is clearly much work to be done still but we hope we have provided a foundation upon which future studies may be based.

We have made no attempt to deal with matters such as the general history of pewter and its origins, how it is made, or its composition, except in so far as particular aspects may be especially relevant to our study. These matters have been well covered in other volumes, some of which are listed in the bibliography, and repetition in a work of this kind would add nothing to its usefulness.

It only remains to record our most grateful thanks to all those collectors, owners and museum officials who have been so generous in their help and in allowing us to examine, record and photograph their pewter (or doing it for us) and to all those individuals, organisations and official bodies who have permitted, and helped us to search for and examine records and documents, old and new. We cannot, unfortunately, name them all, but we must pay particular tribute to members of the Pewter Society for their knowledgeable advice and encouragement, and to the Worshipful Company of Pewterers for the inspiration of their own wonderful collection of British pewter.

There are, however, two people who must receive especial mention. Firstly, Richard Mayne, Vice President of the Société Jersiaise and the author of the standard work entitled "Old Channel Island Silver", as well as of other books on various aspects of Channel Island life and history. He has been our constant adviser on matters of Channel Island lore and history, on where to look and what for, and has himself sought out information, sources, and collections of local pewter; we cannot prize his help too high. The second person to whom we owe a very great debt is Ronald F. Michaelis, the doyen of pewter authors, a Past President of The Pewter Society and himself a Freeman of the Worshipful Company of Pewterers, who has not only most kindly agreed to introduce this work, but also, throughout its long period of gestation, has provided detailed information from his own previous records and researches and been especially generous in giving advice and encouragement and answering many questions from his fund of knowledge.

Jersey, Channel Islands

July 1972

Mr. Michaelis died whilst this book was still under production and we have felt it appropriate to dedicate the work to him.

List of Line Drawings

(By the writer unless otherwise credited)

List of Plates

(all photographs were taken by the writer except where otherwise indicated and credited)

IN TRIBUTE
TO THE MEMORY OF
RONALD F. ('MICK') MICHAELIS
MASTER OF PEWTER
OBIT 28TH MARCH 1973

1 The Background

In our preface we have defined, in general terms, what we mean by 'Channel Islands' pewter – namely a style, pattern or shape, or, more accurately, related groups of shapes, of flagons and measures (see Plates I, LXII, LXIII and LXIV) which are peculiar to the Channel Islands and which were not normally used elsewhere. To this special category we have added other pewter articles used in the Islands, though not necessarily peculiar to them, but made by Channel Islands pewterers. Even so, the list of items involved is still relatively restricted and it must be accepted from the start that Channel Islands pewter is a limited and specialised field. It is, nevertheless, a very interesting and individual one linked to the rather special quality of the life and history of the Islands with characterstics all its own.

Having defined the subject, the next question must be 'How old is it and what is its historical and social background?' Ignoring, for the present, pieces with a date incorporated in the maker's touch, which itself refers generally only to the original date of striking of the touch and to the opening of the maker's own business, the earliest dated Channel Islands piece so far found is a flagon of the largest size, clearly a vessel used for Holy Communion, with the inscription stamped on the lid DONNE A L'EGLISE DE SAIN IEAN 1718, still in the possession of St. John's Parish Church in Jersey. The piece is in the clear style of Jersey pewter in its fully developed form as we now know it and has, stamped on the lid in a small incuse rectangle with chamfered corners, the initials P:D:R. For reasons fully set out later we are satisfied that this piece is the work of a Huguenot pewterer living in Jersey at the time and therefore that the date is genuine.

Clearly, pewter must have been used in the Islands before this time and indeed there are a number of inventories of houses of the second half of the 17th century listing pewter in some quantity – flagons, plates and other useful utensils.* Unfortunately none of the inventories describe the pewter as to type, shape, maker or other characteristic though 'English plates' and a 'Dutch measure' are specifically mentioned.

*There are, in fact, in the Guernsey archives references to pewter vessels and other articles as early as 1500.

Were the flagons and measures then in use of Channel Islands types as we now know them today, or were they French shapes, or English, or some transitional form between? These are questions to be further discussed, but before doing so, we should ask whether the history of Island pewter can be traced still further back to the 16th century or earlier? Unfortunately, so far, this has not been possible; although there are written records of the Islands' history of much earlier date, pewter seems never to have been mentioned – the earliest reference is in a Guernsey law of 1611 to be referred to later – nor are any *recognisable* surviving examples known.

The latter is perhaps not very surprising in view of the comparatively small size and population of the territories. If one considers, for example, how little English pewter is still extant dating from, say, prior to 1600 – mainly spoons and a few pieces of ecclesiastical ware, the latter all 'museum' pieces – then it would not be surprising if the tiny and sparsely populated Islands had preserved nothing which showed the special local characteristics which we now call 'Channel Islands' if those then existed. But it may well have been that these special characteristics had not then been developed, or were only in embryo and that all, or most of the pewter in the Islands was English or French of the patterns current in those countries at that time. Much, possibly all, of this pewter would, in any case, have been destroyed in one way or another, but some pieces may have survived and found their way back to their country of origin, all trace of their former Channel Islands connections having now been lost.

To understand the derivation and development of Channel Islands pewter it is essential to know something of the Islands' life and history and their special situation vis-a-vis both England and France. The Channel Islands, of course, conquered England! At the time of the Battle of Hastings they were part of the Duchy of Normandy and were therefore on the winning side – a fact that has always played a part in the minds and history of Channel Islanders. The Islands have always been, subsequently, especially loyal subjects of the British Crown (except for a brief period during the Commonwealth, mainly in Guernsey), but because of physical propinquity, ease of communications and language ties, links with France, both culturally and physically, were for many centuries, much closer than with England, indeed until the 19th century. Local dialects, descended from Norman and Breton French, are still in use in the Islands today and much of the local seasonal labour, especially for agriculture, still comes from France. French money was the main currency in the Islands until as late as 1830 and Acts of the States and business of the Courts were conducted in the French language even into the 20th century. The life, manners and customs of the Islands have therefore been greatly influenced by France in all spheres: one would expect this influence to include pewter, which in fact, is the case in no small degree.

Reference has already been made to the quantity of pewter in the Channel Islands in the late 17th century; to appreciate this one has only. to study the inventories of a few houses. True these properties generally belonged to the more wealthy, but there is good reason to suppose that many farms throughout the Islands had pewter in quantity and even the smallest dwellings had a few pieces. In the towns, too, there were many taverns, all with pewter in use. To understand the reason for this profusion of pewter, and taverns, it is necessary to consider the social history of the Islands at that time. By and large the inhabitants were poor, living on farming, fishing and knitting, primarily woollen stockings: they had not had an easy time during the Civil War and the Commonwealth, and, although some improvement took place after the Restoration, the threat of war with France, to which they were in such close proximity, and the demands of the militia billeted in the Islands, still allowed them little freedom or wealth.

One of the main products however was cider; Falle,* the historian, reports that early in the 18th century a quarter of the available land of Jersey was occupied by cider-apple orchards and that the Island was a 'sea of cider'. He states that one, M. de Samarez estimated an annual production of 24,000 hogsheads, that is some $1\frac{1}{2}$ million gallons! The population of Jersey at this time was probably about 20,000. Every farm and great house had its cider press and it was undoubtedly the universal drink; indeed, at one time, the import of foreign wines and liquors was prohibited in an effort to protect the cider industry. Some, of course, was exported (at £1.25 per hogshead in the late 17th century) but a very great deal was drunk in the Islands. It was cheap, effective in soothing a man's worries, especially his poverty, and its consumption helped to pass the time, particularly in the winter when there was so little else to do. To keep, transport and drink this vast quantity of cider, quite apart from wine and beer which were also consumed, what better than pewter utensils? The larger Channel Islands flagons are still known by many of the older people as cider jugs, although virtually no cider is now made in the Islands.

The bulk of the pewter vessels in use in the Islands in the 17th century and earlier may well have come from France, but there was also English pewter, either specifically imported or brought over by Royalist refugees, to Jersey particularly, during and after the Civil War. There may also have been pieces from continental countries other than France and indeed one house inventory specifically mentions a Dutch measure.

It is now, however, time to consider the essential characteristics of

*Philip Falle, *Account of Jersey* (1694).

Channel Islands pewter as we know it today, remembering that it is the flagon or measure that is, by and large, the only uniquely local piece.

There are two basic patterns, known as 'Jersey' and 'Guernsey' respectively (see Plate 1), each distinct and usually easily differentiated. However, there is one sub-type which, though clearly attributable primarily to Guernsey, has a very close similarity to the Jersey pattern and, very occasionally, other pieces are found which are not so easily attributable and which may, perhaps, be considered as 'hybrids'.

Even today, more than two centuries after most of them were made, the types are, in the main, found only in their respective Islands: for example, only one out of every ten Channel Islands pieces examined in Jersey was of the Guernsey pattern and even some of these are known to have been brought to the Island relatively recently from either Guernsey or England.

The typical Jersey flagon has a long incurved neck, which, from just above the mid-point between base and lip, begins to swell out in a flowing curve to form a bulbous 'belly'. Beneath the belly, the body curves outwards for a short distance to form a foot rim and is usually finished with a small convex or splayed moulding. The body surface is generally entirely plain with just a single incised line at the top of the base moulding, though some lidded examples do have incised lines at the lip and elsewhere and such lines are not uncommon in the unlidded range. (Fig. 1 shows the salient features of a typical Jersey flagon and its outline as compared with the most usual Guernsey shape.) The lid is

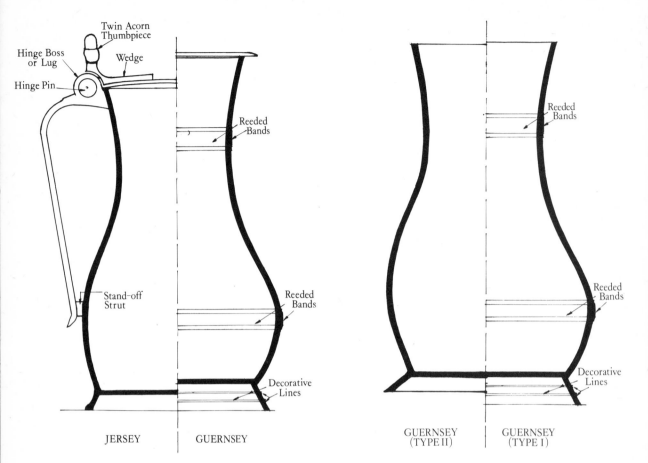

Labels on figure:
Twin Acorn Thumbpiece
Hinge Boss or Lug
Wedge
Hinge Pin
Reeded Bands
Reeded Bands (upper right)
Stand-off Strut
Reeded Bands
Reeded Bands (right)
Decorative Lines
Decorative Lines (right)

JERSEY | GUERNSEY

GUERNSEY (TYPE II) | GUERNSEY (TYPE I)

Fig. 1 Comparative shapes of typical Jersey and Guernsey (Type I) lidded flagons *c.* 1750. (Taken from actual caliper measurements).

Fig. 1A Comparative shapes of Guernsey Types I and II lidded flagons. (Taken from caliper measurements).

*Marks officially struck to indicate that the capacity conforms to the correct standard.

heart-shaped and pointed at the front end to match the rudimentary pouring spout made by pinching the front of the flagon: the thumb-piece (see Fig. 2), consists of two acorns with their axes set at an angle of about 90 degrees on, usually, a single flanged hinge with a wedge or tongue of varying length and width. Occasional examples are found, especially in the smaller sizes, with acorns closer together and, rarely, with a multiple flanged hinge. The handle is straplike and solid and usually offset from the body by a small strut at the foot but there is a significant, though small, group with no strut. This latter variation and differences in the length and width of the wedge, the thickness of the base and other details are believed to have considerable relevance as an indication of date and these factors, and others, will be the subject of detailed examination later. The maker's touch, if present, is usually, but not invariably, inside the lid and in a form not found in English pewter; verification seals* are found on many examples on one or both sides of the lip and of various types and sizes. Owners' initials are generally in the typical Channel Island form, which will be explained later, fairly

18

crudely chiselled or scratched on the handle. Unlidded specimens are of similar basic shape but frequently have a different form of moulding at the foot, whilst the top of the handle is either in the form of an unpierced hinge boss or a curve, either continuous to the lip or stepped at the top. Six sizes of Jersey flagons or measures are known from just under half a gallon Imperial measure (known locally as a pot and pronounced 'po' as in French) to about one ninth of a modern pint, known as a Jersey noggin, made to a local standard fully discussed in a later chapter. Two examples of unlidded measures have, however, been found with an additional 'intermediate' capacity size: these are discussed in a later chapter.

To sum up, the essential features of the Jersey pattern may be considered to be the acorn thumbpiece on a heart-shaped lid allied to the plain, smooth curved shape with a very small base moulding.

There are two quite distinct Guernsey patterns which we shall call Types I and II (see Fig. 1A). The general outline of Type I is more pear-shaped than the Jersey and has a more pronounced belly (see Fig. 1). It has two further features which especially distinguish it, firstly, a deep outward sloping skirt or foot rim, usually decorated with incised lines or mouldings and, secondly, reeded bands of decoration, nearly always at the neck and around the belly, though at the latter point they are sometimes replaced by incised lines. Type II pieces, which generally appear to have the same identification marks on top of the lid,* have almost exactly the basic body shape of a Jersey flagon (see Fig. 1B). Moreover, unlike Type I, they normally have no bands or lines on the body, though they do have a skirt or foot rim. This, however, is set at a 'flatter' angle than in the case of Type I and is sometimes somewhat smaller and rather rudimentary. It will be suggested later that Type I is much earlier than Type II, some examples of which indeed may even be of late 19th century origin. The lid of both types is of a shape similar to the Jersey pattern with the pointed front end over the pinched spout, but the thumbpiece, whilst usually of the twin acorn type, is not infrequently found in the quart size (Type I only), with twin buds, their axes set at a wide angle of 120 degrees or more. Wedges of Type I are different from the Jersey form, usually being narrower and inclined at a steeper angle to the lid, but Type II resemble the Jersey pattern. All the foregoing features are examined in detail and illustrated (Figs. 2 to 7), in Chapter 2. Unlike most of their Jersey brothers, the Guernsey pieces usually have all their information on the TOP of the lid – the maker's touch, after a London form, and the various initials of the owner or dealer, these latter, contrary to the usual Jersey practice, being stamped, usually with individual letter punches, and not roughly chiselled or scratched: a few rare specimens have been found with a touch inside the lid. Handles are

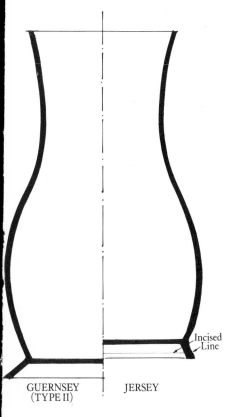

Incised Line

GUERNSEY (TYPE II)   JERSEY

Fig. 1B Comparative shapes of Jersey and Guernsey (Type II) lidded flagons. (Taken from caliper measurements).

*but see Chapters 2 and 5 in regard to certain unmarked pieces of similar style which seem to have been made for Jersey use.

straplike, as on the Jerseys, but differ in detail and, except rarely, have a strut near the terminal. With only one known exception, Guernseys of standard Type I skirted shape do not have Guernsey verification seals; no doubt the reason for this is that, for something like two centuries, they could not legally be used as measures in that Island because all measures of pewter were specifically forbidden under the local Weights and Measures Law of 1611 (presumably to prevent fraudulent practices by denting the relatively soft metal): Guernsey pieces of this Type are therefore properly flagons or jugs. Probably for this reason, too, the range of sizes was limited, only three lidded sizes generally having been made, viz. the pot, or double quart, the quart and the pint. A few very rare half-pints, made by known Type I makers and with most of the Guernsey features, have, however, been found (one, very exceptionally, bears Guernsey verification seals) and also another piece of this size of somewhat similar style, but with certain detail differences. A single half-noggin has also been found which might just possibly be attributed to Guernsey. No unlidded Guernsey pieces are known. Type II Guernseys, however, are frequently found with the Island's verification seals of a rose and a fleur-de-lys on one or both sides of the lip and in this Type the half-pint size has also been found – though rarely.

It is now appropriate to consider where the main Channel Islands shapes come from. Obviously they did not suddenly appear overnight fully developed but, like all art forms, evolved from previous types, either indigenous or foreign and adapted for their required use in accordance with the manners, customs and tastes of the time.

As already stated a pot flagon of the fully developed Jersey pattern, dated 1718, has been found. It seems, therefore, that the initial developments towards a Channel Islands shape and style must have commenced sometime around the year 1700 at the latest, and could possibly have arisen even earlier. Indeed, we must not overlook the possibility of the pattern, or something very like it, having been in use in the Islands for a considerable part of the 17th century. This will be discussed in more detail later in relation to certain particular specimens which have come to our notice. Assuming, however, a date around 1700, or a little earlier, what flagons or measures were being made elsewhere from which the Jersey type, as we know it, could have evolved – bearing in mind the essential features, such as the twin-acorn thumbpiece and wedge, the pinched pourer, the straplike handle and the general outline with long incurved neck and rounded belly?

In England, flagons of the Carolean, Jacobean and early Georgian days tended to be straight and cylindrical, with a variety of thumbpieces and lids, the whole quite unlike the Jersey pattern and clearly contributing nothing to its design. There was, however, the English

11 English baluster measure of quart capacity with ball and wedge thumb-piece, late 16th or early 17th century. (Photo: R. F. Michaelis).

baluster-shaped measure of an earlier period (see Plate 11) which continued to be made well into the 18th century. In shape it resembled the conventional staircase baluster and was therefore not unlike a somewhat flattened Jersey type. However, in its later forms, it usually had a collar at the top, a round instead of a heart-shaped lid and a thumbpiece of the ball, hammerhead, bud or some other type, but not the typical twin-acorns of the Channel Islands, this latter being completely unknown in English pewter: the handles of English baluster measures up to about 1725 were not dissimilar to those on Jersey flagons, being flat and solid. Apart, however, from these very limited similarities, the style and 'feel' of the Channel Islands flagons and measures are quite different from those of the English types then current and, generally, it seems unlikely that they had derived from them. However, one or possibly two rare examples are known of an unusual baluster form, not entirely English, nor, for that matter, entirely consistent with Channel Islands shapes, but with the thoroughly un-English twin-acorn thumbpiece, redolent of the Channel Islands, and, in the author's collection, there is also a virtually identical piece with a twin-bud thumbpiece reminiscent of that found on some Guernsey Type I quarts: these pieces are examined in detail later (see Chapter 5 and Plates XXVII and XXVIII and Appendix V).

If we now consider Continental pewter, especially French, we do find a number of points of similarity with the Channel Islands types, for instance the twin acorn thumbpiece and wedge, the pinched pourer and the long waisted neck, though the rounded belly is less common: the handle too, is of similar shape and profile. Throughout France there was a great proliferation of shapes of flagons, measures and jugs, but those of Normandy exhibit the greatest similarity to the Channel Islands types, as would be expected in the light of the geographical proximity and the historical and trading associations to which reference has already been made. Indeed, French and Channel Islands types are not infrequently confused and a relatively recently published book has a photograph of the more common type of Normandy pichet entitled 'Jersey'. In fact the differences are very plain (see Plate III); firstly, the lower part of the body of the Normandy piece is shouldered and almost cylindrical, though tapering inwards slightly from the vertical towards the base, whereas the typical Channel Islands flagon is of curved baluster shape; secondly the French pichet has a pronounced collar around the neck not found on Channel Island pieces. There are, however, some Normandy types (see Plate IV), which much more resemble the curved Channel Islands shapes, particularly that of the Guernsey pattern, and the Victoria & Albert Museum has a flagon (see Plate V) attributed to Anduze in south-eastern France, of somewhat similar form. French measures or flagons of these types, however, are generally not earlier than the 18th century and we must look still further back for their origins and perhaps for those of the Channel Islands patterns.

There is, in A. G. Verster's book, *Old European Pewter*, a photograph (Plate 16) of a flagon of the 16th century, attributed to Rouen, clearly a forerunner of the Normandy pichet and with several of the characteristics and some of the feeling of the Jersey type. This would be quite apposite and not unexpected in view of the fact that Jersey had close connections with this region and, indeed, the Jersey system of weights was based on the ancient Marc or Standard of Rouen.

There are, however, examples from elsewhere in Europe which seem to have at least some points in common with Channel Islands types. There are, for instance, some Dutch flagons as early as the 16th century, an example of which, a Leyden flagon, appears on page 73 of Cotterell's *Pewter Down the Ages* and in the same volume (page 74) another 16th century flagon, attributed to Breslau, in Silesia, again of a shape reminiscent of the Channel Islands. There are also paintings, particularly by Dutch artists, which clearly show flagons having certain similar

III Normandy Pichet, shouldered type, late 18th century; height to lip 230mm. Note decorated hinge pin boss identical to Jersey Group 4 (see Plate VIIIb).

v Flagon of Anduze (South-eastern France), early 18th century. (By courtesy of the Victoria & Albert Museum).

IV Normandy Pichet, baluster type, town of Falaise, late 18th century; height to lip 260 mm.
(Photo: David Walter-Ellis).

attributes – one *circa* 1650 by Hendrik Sorgh* and a still earlier (*c.* 1490–1520) panel from the Alkmaar Tryptich (see Plate VI). Similar too, in some respects, are some of the measures and flagons of Switzerland.

There is nothing surprising in all these relationships; what tends to be forgotten nowadays is that in those times Europe was genuinely *international*; there was free access, both physically and for the transmission of thought and art between large areas of the Continent without customs or other barriers – indeed, many of today's separate countries were then subject to one monarchy. It was only later in the 17th and still more in the 18th century that nationalism grew, countries became separate and barriers were set up, with the result that types of pewter and other applied art forms became more specific to particular countries.

To return to Normandy, Plate IV shows a typical 18th century flagon of the town of Falaise. Charles Boucaud, in his standard work, *Les Pichets d'Étain*, now unfortunately out of print, has called this baluster-shaped form 'Type II', the more common shouldered form of pichet (Plate III) being his Type I. Similar Type II Normandy shapes are found at Rouen and Lisieux, but generally not elsewhere in north-western France. Most of these pieces have banded decoration and a skirt similar to the Guernsey and the general shape is much more akin to that pattern than to the Jersey. Nearly all have a twin-acorn thumbpiece and wedge similar to the Channel Island flagons and also a heart-shaped lid and 'pinched' pourer. Plate VII shows a delightful small Rouen piece of Type II, but in this instance with a twin-bar thumbpiece not found on Channel Islands flagons.

Whilst we may accept, prima facie, a French, and more specifically a Normandy influence as the direct source of many of the features of the Channel Islands types, and particularly of the Guernsey, we must always bear in mind that the French types themselves were influenced by developments elsewhere and we must also admit the possibility, slight though it may be, of *direct* influence from other countries well before the beginning of the 18th century.

On the assumption that the quite distinctive styles of the Channel Islands were developed basically from French models, why was this so and how, in practice, did it take place? The answers to these questions seem to depend on two factors, firstly, on where most of the pewter in use in the Islands before the development of the special Channel Islands patterns came from and, secondly, on where the Channel Islands style was developed and originally made. As far as the first point is concerned, it seems likely that a large percentage of the flagons, measures and tankards had come from France. A considerable quantity was needed and the close proximity of France and the regular commerce between the Islands and that country, especially with Normandy via the port of

VI Detail from the Aalkmaar Tryptich *c.* 1500: Note flagon in girl's right hand. (By permission of the Rijksmuseum, Amsterdam).
(Photo: C. Arkwright).

*National Gallery No. 1056.

24

Rouen, which even, at times, continued whilst France and England were at war, ensured a steady supply.

As to where the earliest Channel Island types originated and where the pieces themselves were first made, there would appear to be three possible main alternatives, viz: (a) in the Channel Islands, (b) in France or elsewhere on the Continent, or (c) in England.

It should be stressed that these alternatives are directed solely to the *earliest* Channel Islands types. Although currently available evidence suggests that this refers to the Jersey pattern rather than to the Guernsey, both are undoubtedly appreciably earlier than has been credited by previous writers on the subject. In fact, the literature concerning Channel Islands pewter in minimal, being confined almost entirely to brief mentions in books on English pewter and a few articles in periodicals, of which by far the best contribution is the three page essay by Capt. A. V. Sutherland Graeme entitled *Pewter of the Channel Islands* in the *Antique Collector* of May 1938.

Most previous writers on the subject have generally not ventured any opinion as to place of origin, or of manufacture, though some appear to have tacitly assumed it to have been England, whilst others have accepted, without question, that it was the Islands themselves: the conclusive evidence is hard to find. Richard Mayne, in compiling his standard work on Channel Islands silver, searched exhaustively in books, pamphlets, documents, newspapers and every other conceivable source for references to silver makers and dealers and achieved a considerable measure of success. At the same time, being also keenly interested in local pewter, he looked out for any mention of local pewterers, or of vendors of pewter, but not one reference of any kind was found. Our subsequent researches, however, have achieved a small measure of success with the discovery of the arrival in Jersey in 1688, or possibly the previous year, of two Huguenot refugees, who in abjuring the Catholic faith, gave their profession as 'potier d'étain' – that is, 'pewterer' – and the name of the widow of a third French pewterer is also entered in the same list. We believe that one of these two Huguenot pewterers, Pierre du Rousseau, from Châteauneuf, near St. Malo, was the maker of at least three (and probably five) extant flagons, including the St. John's pot dated 1718 and another pot and a quart in the writer's possession, all of which bear the touch P:D:R struck in an incuse rectangle. Furthermore, such information as we have as to his life (see Chapter 6) suggests that we must also accept that, in all probability, he made his pewter in Jersey.

Where the moulds came from, whether du Rousseau himself made them and whether he was the actual 'originator' of the Jersey pattern cannot yet be decided – both may be possible; alternatively he may have acquired the moulds from some pewterer already in the Islands but not yet traced, or may have copied or adapted the design from earlier patterns already circulating in the Island. On the other hand, both the moulds and the original design, or one or the other, may originally have come from outside the Islands, in particular England or France.

Arguments in favour of the manufacture of pewter in the Islands, at a date even earlier than du Rousseau, may be the small but regular shipments of tin, and possibly even unfinished pewter, to the Islands from Cornwall in the second half of the 17th century; the apparently ready purchase in Jersey of prizes of tin captured on their way to France between 1640 and 1650, as reported by Chevalier in his diaries, and the fact that, long before the Revocation of the Edict of Nantes in 1685, indeed ever since the beginning of the persecution of the Huguenots, Protestant refugees from France were arriving in the Islands – often men well educated and skilled in the arts and therefore perhaps capable of producing the designs, moulds, tools and finished pewter articles. The Jersey pattern, therefore, could well have been gradually evolved in the Islands, based on French styles with which the immigrants would have been familiar.

The question of the manufacture of the moulds does present some difficulty; naturally they stem from the design. They were expensive and of great value to the pewterer; indeed by no means all pewterers had them; in England, for example, they were often hired by one pewterer from another; sometimes they were owned by the Guild. Moulds required especial skill in manufacture and were generally made in gunmetal, a heavy alloy of copper and tin with possibly some lead and zinc. For hollowware, such as a lidded flagon, a mould could well consist of some 16 separate sections, each part carefully and accurately made to fit tightly together for casting. It was the mould that really determined the ultimate object, just as today the machine tool is more important than what it produces. It is possible that du Rousseau, a trained pewterer, could have made his own moulds but this would have been unusual: alternatively a French bellfounder is a bare possibility, but from what we know of the local crafts and craftsmen of the time it seems most unlikely that the necessary skill existed amongst the local inhabitants or that there would have been the need for it. A pewterer's tools present less difficulty;

though specialised they could be copied and presumably du Rousseau would have brought over his own with him as any craftsman would have done in such circumstances.

The possibility of French or other continental manufacture seems unlikely for a number of reasons, despite the probable derivation of the basic design. Firstly, the critical period in the development of the Jersey type, assuming it to be the second half of the 17th century, was one of the more difficult times for commerce and intercourse between the Islands and France due to the Anglo/French wars, their inevitable effects on the Islands and fears of invasion. The persecution of the Huguenots and the presence of many of them in the Islands would also inevitably affect the situation. Secondly, the composition of the metal of most Channel Islands pewter seems quite different from that of France of the same period. The former darkens in colour quite quickly, acquires a pronounced and stubborn patina and tends to corrode, especially in the salt laden, humid atmosphere of the Islands. On the other hand, French pichets which have been found in the Islands, having apparently been there for some considerable time, generally seem to remain much brighter and to acquire only a light tarnish or patina, probably indicating a basically different metal composition, containing a greater proportion of lead. There is no doubt that to all appearances the metal of most Jersey flagons has much more the consistency and feel of English pewter than of French. There is not the slightest evidence to suggest that any other Euroean country is worthy of any consideration as the source of supply of early Channel Islands pewter or moulds.

Turning then to the possibility of English manufacture; the metal seems 'right'; the standard of manufacture is almost always excellent and of the best London grade; the style of most of the 'Jerseys' is particularly fine and, clearly, they have been made from high quality moulds and finished by skilled pewterers – all points in favour of English origin. Furthermore, the only other items of pewterware found in the Islands in quantity, plates and chargers, are virtually all by known English makers and carry the normal London touchmarks. The fact that many of what we believe to be the earlier Jersey flagons have no touch at all is not of great significance; by no means all English pewter of the late 17th and early 18th centuries bore touchmarks, despite the fact that various regulations required it to be marked, and, indeed, there seems to have been a period, especially around 1700, when touches were even infrequently struck on flagons and measures. The main difficulty in relation to manufacture in England is to account satisfactorily for the development of the Channel Islands patterns, stylistically quite different from those generally being made by the English pewterers, and derived, we believe, primarily from French originals. Why should pewterers in

London have developed such types and whence derived them?

It is appropriate here to quote from H.H.Cotterell's preface to his book *Pewter Down the Ages*; there will, no doubt, be those who disagree, perhaps strongly, with Cotterell's conclusions and comments, but his enormous research and experience in the subject cannot be lightly passed over. He says '. . . it is not too much to say, that most of the types which up to now have been accepted as *purely British* are in reality, nothing more than local adaptions of well-established European types whose roots are away back in the past, *centuries earlier* than the so-called British types'. It is of course true that there is much more, and more sophisticated, Continental pewter extant of an earlier date than there is British: this is entirely consistent with the progress of all art forms northwards and westwards across Europe, from their beginnings in the Middle East or the Mediterranean countries, both in the Middle Ages and the Renaissance, reaching Britain considerably later and being adapted there in conformity with the life, character and customs of the country.

If one accepts a generalised assumption of this kind, then there would be no reason why Channel Islands types, of patterns in many ways possibly similar to those in use on the Continent perhaps one or more centuries before, should not have been developed in London. However there are other possible explanations: it could be that one or more of the London pewterers, perhaps of Channel Islands origin, or with Channel Island connections (for example already selling plates there), knowing local conditions in the Islands and the large amount of pewter in use, decided that this was a market well worthy of special consideration, especially as the French, who had probably provided most of the flagons and measures in the past, were now very unpopular in the Islands following the war, the continued threats of invasion and the persecution of the Huguenots. They would also know that the Islanders were very conservative and, although strong supporters of the English crown, would perhaps not find the typical English pieces of the period to their liking, but would want something with a fair resemblance to what they had been accustomed to in the past. However English pewterers would have been most unlikely, and unwilling, to copy French patterns exactly, especially in this time of war or uneasy peace and against a background of centuries of mutual animosity. It is therefore reasonable to suppose that they would have adopted a compromise using the more obvious French, and therefore traditional Channel Islands features, such as the acorn thumbpiece (believed in the Islands to act as a protection against thunderbolts), the heart shaped lid and general character, but incorporating their own ideas of a more gracious and smoothly curved body, perhaps 'after' the English baluster or some of the earlier Continental pieces. However, if this were so, we may well wonder why they did not, apparently, market these designs in England.

In the present state of our knowledge, therefore, the position can only be summed up as follows:

(i) there is a high degree of probability that at least some flagons were made in Jersey in the first few years of the 18th century – and possibly even in the last decade of the 17th century – by Pierre du Rousseau and perhaps others,

(ii) du Rousseau may have originated the design and made the first moulds or had them made to his order (either in the Islands or England) or he may have taken them over from some pewterer previously operating in the Islands,

(iii) it is possible that a form of Channel Islands or Jersey style existed even as early as the middle of the 17th century.

(iv) despite the acceptance of France as the place of derivation of the basic design of the Channel Islands types, it is most improbable that any Channel Islands pewter or moulds were made there at this period, and

(v) the very earliest examples, and moulds, could have originated in London, more particularly if (iii) above is true, despite the clear French influence on the patterns and the probable manufacture of some early examples in Jersey.

So far, in our search for the origins of Channel Islands pewter, we have concentrated on Jersey on the assumption that the Guernsey pattern came later. Our reasons for this assumption are basically twofold. Firstly, most of the Guernsey flagons of the earlier Type I so far found are by English makers recorded in Cotterell's 'Old Pewter' and with dates well into the 18th century. It is true that we have found a few pieces – one piece in the Seigneurial pewter of Sark – with the date of 1706 in the touch of a member of the Ingles family. However the date refers to the year of the first striking of the touch and is not necessarily in any way related to the actual date of manufacture of the piece itself, although it seems likely that the Sark piece was made before 1726. Secondly, the general style and characteristics of the Guernsey flagons of Type I – the earlier of the two types – are such that any date much earlier than the first quarter of the 18th century seems unlikely. In this connection it is interesting to note that Boucaud* has indicated that the number of similar, baluster-shaped Normandy pieces, which can be definitely identified, by marks, as belonging even to the 18th century, is quite limited and that the majority are probably of 19th century origin.

In later Chapters and Appendices we shall provide as much factual information as possible – as well as further conjecture – and hope that both will assist and stimulate further interest and research into the subject and, in particular, into the problems which we have posed.

*Charles Boucaud, *Les Pichets d'Étain* (1958), Librarie Legueltel, Paris.

2 Lidded Flagons

Detail Characteristics and their Significance

In the last chapter Channel Island pewter was defined and described in broad terms and, at the same time, an attempt was made to establish its origins and to relate it to a social and historical background.

In several instances reference was made to certain details of shape and design and it was suggested that variations or changes in particular features might have some relevance to either dates or makers. In this chapter, therefore, we shall, in addition to considering the general form and shape, look at each separate component of the lidded flagon and attempt to discuss and analyse its salient features or development in some detail. The aim will be to provide clear factual information from the large number of examples actually examined and measured, and to try to relate certain combinations of details to one another and to the chronological development of the flagon: the unlidded measure will be similarly treated in a separate chapter.

The features to be considered comprise (i) the thumbpiece, (ii) the wedge attached to the thumbpiece, (iii) the lid, (iv) the hinge pin, (v) the handle and its method of fixing, (vi) the skirt or bottom moulding, (vii) any decoration or special features and (viii) the general shape.

Before carrying out this detailed examination, however, it is both possible and helpful to identify certain basic groupings which occur within the Jersey and Guernsey styles. Reference has already been made to the fact that there are two distinct types of Guernsey flagons which we have designated Types I and II, the former being the more traditionally known Guernsey and, we believe, the earlier type, and the latter – mostly bearing the initials Ns L Ct on the lid – approximating more to the Jersey pattern: a few of this type may indeed have been made for the Jersey market. In considering detailed characteristics later in this chapter, references embrace both Types unless specific mention is made to the contrary.

Jersey flagons can be divided broadly into four Groups, viz:
Group 1, which includes:

(a) those with the initials P:D:R (see Plate LIV), or with some other mark or device *on top of* the lid which may or may not, in every case, be a maker's mark. We exclude from this Group, however, those few pieces bearing on top of the lid the recorded 'leopards' touch of John de St. Croix, which are included in Group 3. (See note in Chapter 6 as to the Channel Islands spelling of this pewterer's name, i.e. 'Jean de Ste. Croix').

(b) generally those with no marks at all, other than, perhaps, owner's initials crudely scratched on the handle, *but excluding Group 4.*

Group 2, comprising basically those with the maker's initials IN struck inside the lid (Plate LVII), but including an occasional piece of identical characteristics without the touch.

Group 3, those with the initials IDSX struck inside the lid or the recorded 'leopards' touch of John de St. Croix struck either inside or on top of the lid (Plate XI), and

Group 4, those with no touchmark at all but having certain special features, notably, very frequently, a large (15 mm diameter) 'dahlia' boss on one side of the hinge pin (Plate VIII). This appears to be a relatively small Group.

The reason for grouping together two apparently different types in Group 1 will, we hope, become clear when we discuss their closely related detail characteristics, but it is essential that one important reservation be entered about sub-Group 1 (b). Strictly this sub-Group applies most consistently only to the sizes of pot and quart, as there are many un-marked examples in the smaller sizes, and an occasional large piece, which, there is good reason to believe, were made by the makers of Groups 2 or 3, but which were not struck with their touch.* However, as 'pots' and 'quarts' comprise almost three quarters of all lidded flagons found (and some smaller sizes often have their lids missing so that touch identification is not possible), sub-Group (b) may fairly be regarded as representative, provided that care is exercised in checking unmarked examples, particularly in the smaller sizes, and comparing them with the especially significant characteristics which we hope to show relate generally to Group 1. If they do not conform to those characteristics, then comparison with examples analysed in Appendix I may enable them to be ascribed with reasonable certainty to Group 2,* 3 or 4.

References in the following text apply to all Groups unless otherwise indicated.

*An example of this kind of piece, of the pot size, is described in detail in Chapter 7.

The typical thumbpiece of Channel Islands flagons (or lidded measures) consists, as we have seen, of twin acorns set at an angle of 90 degrees (see Fig. 2): the type is very similar indeed to that found on many French, Swiss and other continental examples.

Thumbpiece

31

a

b

VIII

a. Jersey Group 4 quart lidded flagon,
late 18th century.

b. Detail of decorative hinge pin boss.

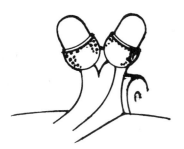

Fig. 2 Typical Channel Islands twin-acorn thumbpiece.

There is a considerable variation in the style, shape and manufacture of the acorns, particularly in the case of Jersey flagons. Some are quite naturalistic, circular in section, and well made, others are more elliptical on plan and sometimes even quite crudely formed: the lower cups of some examples are quite prickly, whereas those of others are entirely smooth – not, apparently, due to wear. These cups, also, on many thumbpieces, of both Jersey and Guernsey flagons, are flattened at the back: this flattening may, in some cases, have been caused merely by continual impact with the top of the handle on opening, or it may have been done deliberately in manufacture, perhaps to allow the lid to 'seat' better when opened. Generally, the whole thumbpiece is erect and at right angles to the lid, but an occasional specimen is found with the thumbpiece tilted forward (see Plate XXVI). No special significance has yet been attached to this variant and it is possible that it may have been due to manufacturing error or subsequent damage.

As would be expected, there is a range of sizes of the acorns corresponding in some degree to the size of the lid and flagon. The acorn thumbpiece seems to have been cast integrally with the wedge, so that differences in the wedge length and width, which we believe have some relevance to date of manufacture, may also reflect differences in the style of the acorns.

So far only one different type of thumbpiece has been found associated with Channel Islands flagons, namely the 'twin-bud', set at a wide angle (see Fig. 3); this has been found on all Type I* Guernsey quarts except those of Wingod, and may exist in other sizes – no Jersey examples have been found with this thumbpiece. Although we have adopted the term 'twin-bud' for this thumbpiece in deference to existing nomenclature in England and France, it is, in fact, unlike the thumbpiece to which that name is applied in those countries, being generally quite smooth and of rather indeterminate shape, but resembling most closely, perhaps, a pair of fruit pips or small stones, such as those of a cherry, joined at the pointed end. They are invariably set at a much wider angle that the twin-acorns – at least 120°. Very occasionally an example is found with traces of 'prickles' on the surface of the buds. (Plate ix shows some varieties of Channel Islands thumbpieces).

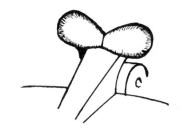

Fig. 3 Twin-bud thumbpiece found on some Guernsey Type I quarts.

Wedges are of various lengths, widths and shapes; the Jersey types (Fig. 4) are generally longer, broader and of more uniform thickness than the Guernsey. In length the former seem to be readily divisible into groups, which can be identified very closely with the 'touch Groups' already mentioned. It is most convenient, initially, to examine the pot because it is in this size that the greatest number of good lidded specimens still exist and thus a wider basis of comparison and assessment is possible.

Pots of Group 1 (see Page 30) generally have wedges of between 51 mm and 56 mm in length (measured from the back of the lid), though one very occasionally finds a specimen with a somewhat shorter wedge which may belong to this Group. Pots of Group 2 (i.e. those flagons which usually have the mark IN inside the lid) have been found only with wedges of 36 mm to 37 mm. The pieces of Group 3 are much more variable; pots with de St. Croix's 'leopards' mark have wedges of 55 mm in length, that is about the same length as those on the flagons of Group 1, but those with his IDSX touchmark usually have relatively short wedges between 27 mm and 32 mm, though an occasional specimen, perhaps one in ten, is found with a longer tongue. Similar groupings appear to apply, though not perhaps to as marked a degree, in the quart size, but in the smaller sizes insufficient lidded examples have been found to form any definite conclusions. In any case, the reservations in regard to the groupings of these smaller sizes, already mentioned earlier in this Chapter in connection with sub-Group 1(b), must always be carefully borne in mind. Flagons of Group 4 seem to have wedges of fairly consistent length, as all of the specimens that we have examined in both pot and quart sizes have varied only between about 34 mm and 38 mm.

Wedge

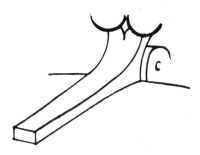

Fig. 4 Typical Jersey wedge.

---

*see page 19.

IX

a. Typical Jersey and Guernsey twin-acorn thumbpiece.

b. Widely spaced twin-acorns, found mainly on Guernsey Type 1 pints.

c. Conjoined twin-acorns, usually found only on smaller sized Jersey flagons.

d. Twin-bud thumbpiece, found on most Guernsey Type 1 quarts.

e. Multiple flanged hinge—a rare variant found on both 'Jerseys' and 'Guernseys' (see Page 40).

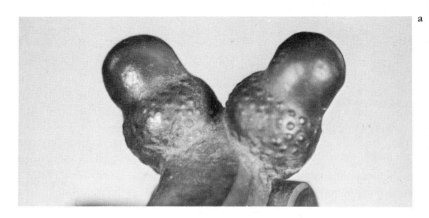

a

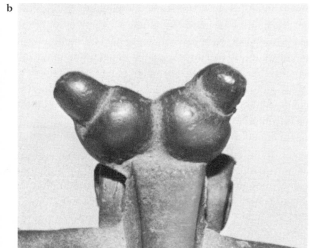

b

c

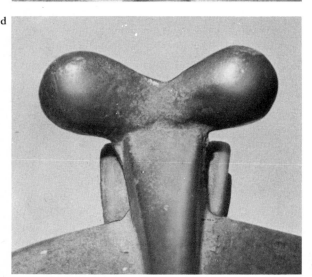

d

e

34

The longer wedges seem generally to be associated with well-made acorns having a circular top and quite closely modelled on the genuine article. The somewhat 'debased' variants of shape and form of thumb-piece, already referred to, appear to occur generally on pieces with shorter wedges and, particularly, on flagons of the smaller sizes not bearing any touchmark. Indeed, on some of the latter pieces the acorns are quite crudely formed and converge indeterminately at the centre.

Boucaud, in his exhaustive study, *Les Pichets d'Étain* noted similar variations in shape and angle on French twin-acorn thumbpieces, in particular on Normandy flagons, between the 17th and 19th centuries, and concluded that the shape became malformed and the acorns converged as time went on. However, we have not, so far, been able to establish that similar variations of form in Jersey thumbpieces (such variations are much less apparent on Guernsey flagons) indicate any precise chronological sequence: indeed, in the case of Group 4, which we believe to be of relatively late date, the thumbpieces are always very well formed with 'prickly' acorn cups.

It is not only in length that the wedge, or 'tongue', of Jersey flagons varies: there is also quite a range of variations in width and shape. Generally, however, the pot size has a maximum width of about 12 mm, on some examples almost constant in width throughout, and on others tapering to about 9 mm. The quart wedge averages about 7 mm in width, again sometimes tapering. Usually the wedges have fairly sharp edges but occasionally they are chamfered.

A particular feature of the Jersey wedge (see Fig. 5), is that it nearly always descends in a curve from the base of the acorns, and thereafter maintains a fairly uniform 'thickness' throughout: a few of the Group 1 pieces, however, including those with du Rousseau's touch, have wedges slightly up-tilted at the front, while an occasional piece has been found, particularly of Group 3, with a wedge diminishing in thickness towards the front rather like the Guernsey.

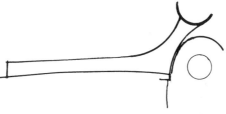

Fig. 5 Side view of typical Jersey wedge. Note generally even thickness with curve up to the base of the acorns.

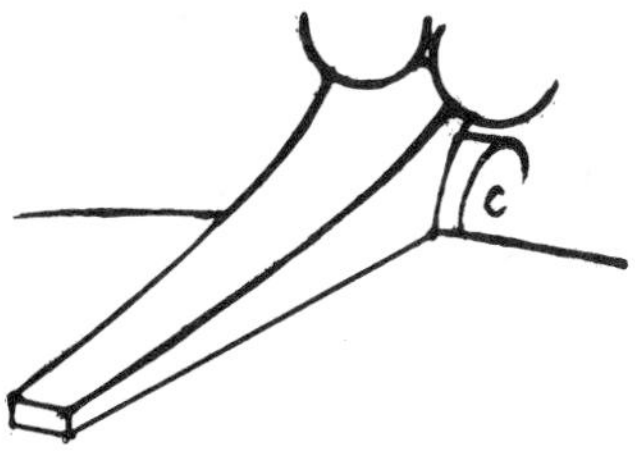

Fig. 6 Typical wedge of Guernsey Type I flagons.

Wedges on Type I Guernsey flagons (Fig. 6) appear to be much more consistent in length than in the case of the Jersey; in the pot size they are usually about 37 mm in length and in the quart and pint only a little less. They are narrower, about a maximum of 10 mm in the largest size, and taper sharply to as little as 4 mm, again with only slight variations in

Fig. 7 Side view of typical wedge on Guernsey Type I flagons. Note nearly straight slope and diminishing thickness.

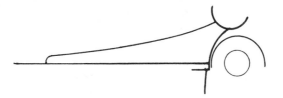

the smaller sizes: the edges are almost always fairly sharp and not chamfered.

The particular feature of the usual Guernsey Type I wedge, in contrast to most Jerseys, is that it slopes quite sharply in almost a straight line from the base of the thumbpiece to the lid and thus becomes progressively 'thinner'. In some cases it almost disappears directly into the lid at the front. (See Fig. 7).

Type II Guernseys, however, have wedges very like the Jersey pattern, i.e. curving down from the thumbpiece instead of in a straight slope, with much less taper, of more even thickness and sometimes with chamfered, instead of sharp edges.

Lid

Lids call for relatively little comment: they have been described as heart-shaped, though leaf-shaped is probably a better definition, (see Plates XXX and LVII).

The Jersey and Guernsey types basically differ little: it should however, be noted that the Guernsey lid 'overlaps' the top of the flagon more than the Jersey, this being especially apparent in the pint size. The distance from hinge to lip in any size is almost always about the same as the maximum width. The Jersey type is usually slightly domed with the pointed lip turned down over the pinched front of the vessel, though some specimens from Group 1 have been found with a flat, or even a slightly concave surface and some of Group 2 are nearly flat. The Guernsey Type I lid is almost always flat, but that on the Type II is normally domed as in the Jersey pattern, which this flagon so much resembles in other ways. Marks on the lid, and elsewhere, such as touches, verification seals, owner's initials, etc. will be considered later.

Hinge Pin

Between 25% and 30% of all lidded Jersey flagons examined had some mark or decoration on one side of the hinge pin, usually on the right side, looking from the handle forward. Figure 8 shows a series of these marks: No. 1 is quite straightforward and is clearly another representation of the initials of John de St. Croix (see Chapter 6) and has been only found on pieces with the IDSX touch inside the lid. Nos. 2, 2A to 6 inclusive and No. 10 have also appeared only on IDSX pieces:* No. 7, in slightly varied form, has been found both on IDSX pieces and on some unmarked examples: No. 8 mainly on those with IN under the lid,

*Cotterell, (*Old Pewter*), illustrates, under John de St. Croix, a further Hinge Pin variety, similar to No. 8 but with the letters IDSX, one in each of the four quadrants: we have seen no example of this.

MARK No.

1

2

2A

3

4

5

6

7 Section

8

9

10

Fig. 8 Marks on hinge pins of Jersey flagons.
NOTE–these marks are generally cast in low relief, except for No. 7, which is conical as shown in section on the right, and No. 9, which is in the form of a large boss, cast in high relief.

but also on a few pieces with no touch, and No. 9 only on Group 4 (with no touch) and also on certain Normandy pieces. It has not, so far, been possible to attach any special significance to these marks and it may be that some were intended merely as decoration. No marks have been found on the hinge pins of Guernsey flagons.

Handle

Handles on all lidded flagons, of both Jersey and Guernsey, are basically the same shape, that is, strap like, but there are considerable differences in size and detail. The Jersey handle, on the pot size, is about 20 mm in width at the top, generally tapering to about 16 mm at the bottom, with a slightly out-turned terminal. It is about 3 mm thick at the centre but rounded off a little on the inside towards the edges, thus providing a more comfortable grip (see Fig. 9). Similar shapes, but proportionally narrower and thinner, are found on the smaller Jersey lidded pieces.

The Type I* Guernsey pots, however, have a handle about 15 mm wide at the maximum and with somewhat less taper towards the lower end, but, right at the bottom, a spade-like widening out over the strut, or joint with the body, is frequently found (see Fig. 10); the terminal is generally slightly less out-turned than the Jersey.

*See page 19.

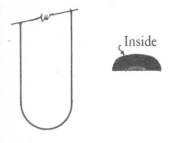

Fig. 9 Jersey handle—rear view and section.
Fig. 10 Guernsey (Type I) handle—rear view and section.

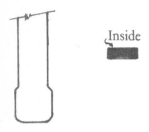

The Guernsey Type I handle is also virtually flat both sides, instead of being rounded inside, as in the Jersey type, and is very slightly thinner, but the handles of Type II follow the Jersey shape. Again the smaller Guernsey sizes have handles similar to that on the pot size, but proportionally narrower and thinner.

The top of the handle in all sizes, both of Jersey and Guernsey, is nearly always two-flanged to accommodate the single-flange hinge of the lid. However, a very few examples, all pints or half-pints, have been found, of both Jersey and Guernsey types, with five-flanged hinges (i.e. three on top of the handle and two on the lid) (see Plate IX), including some by known makers such as de St. Croix and Wingod. The handle is secured to the body at the top by a 'thumb-print' fixing. The so-called 'thumb-print' is caused by the wet 'stopping rag', which is held inside the neck whilst the molten alloy is poured into the handle mould, the handle mould being placed in position on the already cast (and cold) body. At the bottom of the handle there is a variation which is considered to be important from the point of view of date. This variation is that, whilst the majority have the handle connected to the body through a small stand-off strut (see Fig. 1), a relatively few examples have been found with the handle fixed direct to the body, or virtually so. When studying this feature careful examination is necessary to ensure that the original form has not been altered by later refixing or soldering.

Early examples of English pewter baluster measures are usually found with the handle affixed direct to the body near to the lower terminal: it was only later, say about the end of the 17th century, that the stand-off strut appeared and this lasted until lidded measures virtually ceased to be made around the 1780s, though the strut continued for a while on unlidded types until again superseded eventually by direct fixing to the body, though of a different form. It therefore seems entirely credible, especially in the light of other evidence, that a similar development took place in Channel Islands pewter, with the earlier examples having no struts or only very rudimentary ones. The strut is usually cylindrical and quite small, but in the case of Guernsey Type II it is oval or oblong and larger.

Foot Rim, Skirt or Base Moulding

The general shapes of the foot rim, skirt or base mouldings of the Jersey and Guernsey types have already been briefly described. Properly speaking the Jersey has no distinct skirt or foot rim, but merely a small convex or splayed moulding, usually with a single incised line at its top, which serves to raise the bottom of the flagon off the table (see Fig. 11). As such, it, and the well beneath the flagon are of minimum depth, about 7 mm only in the pot size and proportionally smaller in the others. The thickness of the metal forming this moulding is, in the majority of pots,

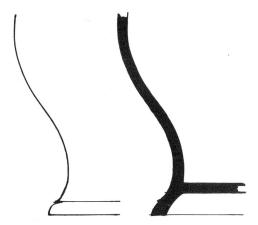

Fig. 11 Typical base moulding on Jersey flagons of Groups 1, 2 and 3. (a) Elevation, (b) Section.

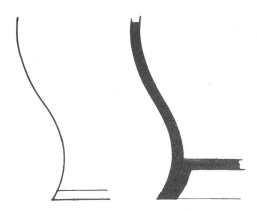

Fig. 12 Typical base moulding on Jersey Group 4 flagons. (a) Elevation, (b) Section.

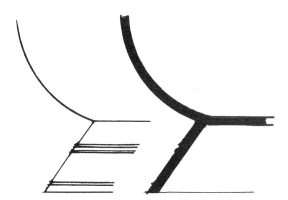

Fig. 13 Typical skirt on Guernsey Type I flagons. (a) Elevation, (b) Section.

about 3 mm; however, some examples have been found with what we have termed a 'thick' base rim of 5 mm or more – easily discernible and distinguishable. Moreover, it has been found, in virtually all cases, that flagons with this really thick base are those with the long wedge and, usually, without a handle strut (which we have assigned to Group 1). The same situation appears to apply in the quart size but we have not found sufficient examples of the smaller sizes to enable us to establish a clear similar trend. A somewhat thicker than normal base is also found on Group 4 pieces, though of a slightly different shape (Fig. 12). A very few flagons, of otherwise general Jersey form and detail, have been found with a small but quite noticeable rather flattened skirt. They appear to be identical in shape to the Type II Guernsey (see below), but all have been found in Jersey and conform to Jersey capacities, and none bear the normal Guernsey Type II marks (the initials Ns L Ct etc.) on the lid. Similarly we have found a very few pieces with certain Guernsey characteristics, especially three half-pints by a known 'Guernsey' maker, but with a Jersey type foot and, in some cases, rather more akin to the Jersey shape. Some of these pieces are discussed further in Chapter 5.

The skirt or foot rim of the Type I Guernsey flagon (Fig. 13) is much more pronounced, to such an extent that it affects the whole style of the piece; it is generally a straight splay outwards from the bottom of the main belly and has the effect of raising the flagon (and creating a well underneath) of about 22 mm in the pot size and proportionally less in the other sizes. The skirt is almost always decorated with one or more lines, sometimes only lightly incised, but more often quite deeply engraved. The metal of the skirt is thinner than that of the Jersey base and there do not appear to be any really significant variations in thickness except from size to size.

On Type II flagons the skirt (when present) is set at a much more acute angle than Type I (see Fig. 1A), is usually not as deep and is often decorated with just a single incised line. However, as we shall see in Chapter 5, some examples lack the typical, almost straight Guernsey skirt and have instead only a rudimentary or ill-formed foot rim (see Fig. 27).

Decoration and Special Features

As has been previously stated, the majority of Jersey lidded flagons – and in this chapter we are dealing solely with the lidded pieces – have only a single, lightly incised line at the base. However, examples have been found with additional, and deeper, engraved lines, often in pairs, at the lip, around the neck, at the belly and just above the base moulding. One or two examples have also been found with a perceptible swelling, or even a projecting fillet, around the neck, possibly concealing a joint. All the examples so far found with these additional features in the pot and quart sizes (and probably in the smaller sizes too) belong either to Group 1 or to Group 4: flagons of the latter Group, in particular, appear always to be decorated – usually with two lines at the lip, one at the bottom of the neck, two below the belly and one just above the base.

Guernsey flagons of Type I, on the other hand, *invariably* have bands of decoration, usually consisting of three raised bands (one wide between two narrow) around the neck and a similar treatment around the belly, though here they are not infrequently replaced with incised parallel lines, usually between five and ten in number and close together: a very occasional specimen has bands at the neck only. The large skirt or foot rim is also almost invariably decorated with a number of lines. Type II Guernseys, however, rarely have any body decoration and the skirt normally has only one incised line, or is sometimes even quite plain.

40

Chronological Conclusion   We have now considered the individual sections of the lidded flagon with the exception of the body shape: it is clear that in the Jersey type a consistent general pattern emerges, namely that there is a group, synonymous with our Group 1, whose special characteristics are a long wedge (of 51 mm to 56 mm in the pot size), well formed acorns for the thumbpiece, a handle fixed directly to the body at the foot, or almost so, and a 'thick' base; also many of the examples in this Group have additional decoration in the form of engraved lines generally not found in Groups 2 and 3, though again appearing in Group 4. Furthermore, these pieces usually seem to be of rather more solid construction than those in Groups 2 and 3 and occasionally, particularly in the quart size, the general shape of the lower section of the body seems slightly straighter and less rounded. Occasionally, also, they have clearly visible body section joints, these latter being invariably horizontal, as they have been on all Channel Islands pieces we have seen.*

In the light of these stylistic characteristics and the date (1718) of the St. John's flagon, which exhibits most of them, our Group 1 can be regarded, with fair certainty, as comprising the earliest fully 'Jersey' flagons of which we have knowledge at the present time. The absence of any verification seals (other than possibly, in very rare cases, one clearly appertaining to, and struck at a much later date) may also be significant; this will be discussed in a later chapter.

It is possible to suggest an approximate date for this Group of flagons: we have identified the maker of the St. John's piece as a Huguenot pewterer who was in Jersey from 1688 until his death in 1729. Because of the detail correlation of nearly all the pieces in this Group, it seems, for all practical purposes, reasonable, on present evidence, to assign to the Group as a whole a date range coincidental with the probable working life of this pewterer in Jersey, say from about 1690 to 1725 or perhaps even up until his death. We hope to show, in considering Groups 2 and 3, particularly the latter, that this is a chronologically reasonable assumption in the light of the stylistic details and documentary evidence relating to those Groups. We must make it clear that, *in this Chapter*, we are considering the unmarked pieces of Group 1 purely from a chronological point of view. Who the makers were we do not know. In Appendix I, however, we have set out full details of pieces examined which we consider to belong to this 'chronological' Group, and in a foreword to the Appendix, we have speculated about the pewterers involved, as to how many there may have been and about the moulds they used.

Next in chronological order after Group 1 come, almost certainly, the flagons of Group 2, that is, primarily those with the touch of IN inside the lid† – a maker so far not specifically identified, but discussed later in the chapter dealing with makers of Channel Islands pewter. In

---

*but see Chapter 5 re vertical jointing of certain rare pieces of English baluster form, but with some Channel Islands characteristics.

---

†but including, possibly some unmarked specimens (see Chapter 7).

x Jersey Group 2 lidded flagon of pot size, maker IN, *c.* 1730.

the pot size, at least, these are the most elegant of all Jersey flagons, being about 6 mm taller than most others and of particularly graceful shape (see Plate x). The wedge length is 36–37 mm, shorter than on the Group 1 pieces, but longer than on most of those in Group 3.

The thumbpieces of these flagons, generally, have nicely finished, circular acorns with well-defined lower cups, usually quite 'prickly', and at least a small strut at the foot of the handle. A factor that strongly supports an earlier dating for this Group than for Group 3 is that, as far as we can tell, they invariably (except possibly for an occasional specimen without a touch) have a verification seal of a type which is judged to be the earliest found, probably of the end of the reign of George I and certainly in use in the earlier years of George II (see Chapter 4), stamped on the left side of the lip, looking from the handle forward. Sutherland Graeme, in what is virtually the only detailed article published on Channel Islands pewter, implied that this form of early mark is *always* on the left side, but, although this has been found to be the case in Group 2, it is not always so in Group 3. It has been found impossible to date these Group 2 flagons with certainty, but in the light of the evidence at present available, their stylistic character and their relationship to Groups 1 and 3, a date range of 1725 to 1740 is suggested.

As to where these flagons and their moulds were made we have no positive evidence. Whilst we have accepted the near certainty that Pierre du Rousseau made his pieces in Jersey (and this may also be true of some at least of the other Group 1 pieces), the case of IN is not a parallel one, if only by reason of the relatively large number of his pieces still existing (though they are still quite scarce in comparison with those of Group 3). Moreover, they are always well made, many of the highest quality, which is by no means always the case with those of Group 1, which sometimes tend to be somewhat 'primitive'. Clearly whoever he was, IN was a most accomplished pewterer with access to good moulds. Whilst it is still thought possible that he manufactured in Jersey, England also is quite feasible.

Wherever made, particularly if in England, it seems necessary to ask, (a) why a touchmark with plain bold initials was used, so unlike the English touches of the period, and, (b) why it was struck inside the lid, a location not used by English pewterers on their own flagons and measures of the period; English pieces were usually 'touched' either near the top of the neck, or inside the bottom of the vessel. The same queries arise in the case of the Group 3 flagons where again the touch, IDSX, is struck boldly inside the lid.

A perfectly logical explanation relates to the already long established Channel Islands custom, and system, of syllabic 'initialling'. Initials were, and are, important in the social life of the Islands: they almost always appear somewhere carved on the granite corner-stones or the lintels of old houses, and on many new ones; frequently over the entrance door one finds the initials of the husband and wife, using her maiden name, with a heart or some other motif between. They appear on locally made silver and there are very few pewter flagons in existence which, whether they have a maker's touch or not, do not carry the initials of an owner somewhere on them.

This system of initialling used seems unique to the Islands; from some time early in the 17th century it became the custom to use not only the initial letter of the Christian name (there was usually only one) and of the surname, but to add, also, the first letter of the second or subsequent syllables of the surname, thus IMG would indicate Jean Mauger. Because this form was used and because the surname frequently contained two syllables or was accompanied by the French 'le' or 'de', three, or even four initials are usually found (e.g. ILCN for Jean le Cornu), and two only quite rarely.

In the light of this old established, and virtually universal, custom in the Islands, what more likely than that a pewterer making in, or exporting to Jersey would also use his initials boldly in the style to which the Islands were accustomed? But why inside the lid? Actually this is the logical place; to strike large, deeply cut touches, such as those of IN and IDSX, a flat surface, which could be placed solidly on an anvil would be almost essential. The handle if used would be liable to be damaged in the striking and would be too narrow on the smaller sizes of flagons: in any case, the maker would, no doubt, be aware that the owner would most likely wish to put his own initials there – it is where they are almost invariably found on Jersey pieces. If the touch were placed in the bottom of the flagon used (as they commonly were) for cider, wine or beer, it would very soon become illegible; thus the lid, surely, is the obvious place, made all the easier, too, because the mark could be struck thereon before attachment to the body by the simple hinge pin.

Faced with the choice of striking his mark inside or outside the lid, the 'Jersey' pewterer, except rarely, preferred the former, perhaps so that, although not spoiling the external appearance, his initials could always be seen as soon as the lid was opened – as no doubt it frequently was – thus keeping his mark literally in the public eye. The makers of Guernseys, on the other hand, for reason unknown, normally used the top surface of the lid. Although generally, so far as Type I is concerned, their touches were less heavily struck and less bold, nevertheless the practice of top striking has, in the writer's view, detracted appreciably from the appearance of some Guernsey pieces.

We now turn to the flagons of Group 3, i.e. those with the mark IDSX inside the lid, or with the 'leopards' touch (Plate XI), either inside *or*

xi 'Leopards' touch of John de St. Croix inside lid of Jersey Group 3 flagon (also found struck on top of lid).

on top. This is by far the largest Group of Jersey lidded flagons, comprising more than half of the total found. It has always been accepted that pieces which bear either of these touches were made by John de St. Croix, a Jerseyman and a pewterer of London, made a Freeman of the Worshipful Company of Pewterers in 1729. The IDSX mark found inside the lid of these flagons, however, is not that which was struck by de St. Croix on the London Touchplate in 1730: that touch is a shield with three lions passant gardant resembling the Jersey coat of arms, surrounded by his full name, JOHN DE ST. CROIX, within a scroll. This has been found on only a few flagons, struck sometimes on top of the lid and sometimes inside (see Plate xi), but it is the invariable touch on de St. Croix's plates so far as we have been able to discover. Without the slightest doubt, however, the initials IDSX do, according to Channel Islands custom, stand for John (or Jean) de St(e). Croix and it is surely carrying coincidence or supposition too far to suggest that this mark can be other than that of the same John de St. Croix who was the known London pewterer.

Accepting this premise, Group 3 flagons could, therefore, theoretically, have been made any time from 1729 onwards. In the chapter on the pewterers' lives we shall examine more closely possible alternative dates and places of manufacture and shall suggest that, in all probability, the latest date was 1765. Here we need note only that there are variations, not in capacity alone, which could perhaps be fairly easily explained, but also in wedge length, details of acorns, hinge pin decoration, etc., which

44

may indicate some chronological sequence, which we have not yet elucidated.

Group 4 flagons have only comparatively recently been recognised as forming a quite separate Group with particular and quite consistent characteristics. The most easily distinguishable features appear to be:

(a) a large decorated boss on one end of the hinge pin, resembling, to some extent, a dahlia flower (see Fig. 8 and Plate VIII). The boss is situated on the right hand side of the flagon, looking from the handle forward, and has been found on all pot and quart size specimens assigned to this Group. In the smaller sizes, pieces apparently belonging to this Group have also frequently been found with an extra boss on the end of the hinge pin, but undecorated,

(b) a series of incised lines around the vessel as already described on pages 43 and 44, usually at the lip, the base of the neck and below the belly, and

(c) a form of base rim different from that found on any of the other three Jersey Groups (see Fig. 12).

All the examples of this Group seem to be well-made, are still in excellent condition and with no more than a relatively light, sometimes greenish, patina. The general shape, form of handle (with strut), lid, wedge and thumbpiece are all typically 'Jersey' and the acorns are very well-formed, naturalistic and with prickly cups. The finish of the whole piece is usually smooth and silky and most examples show evidence of substantial machine finishing. One unusual feature is that they generally seem to lack owner's initials, a rare occurrence in Jersey pewter. The peculiar, large, decorative hinge pin boss has also been found, in absolutely identical form, on certain Normandy pieces, i.e. typical shouldered pichets of early 19th century, or possibly late 18th century, origin (see Plate III) and on a vase-shaped, lidded jug, certainly of the 19th century (see Fig. 14). The appearance and condition of the Jersey pieces definitely suggests a similar age to the Normandy pieces and, in the absence of any touchmark or any contrary evidence, we would date these flagons between 1790 (or possibly a little earlier) and, say, 1830. The evidence of the Normandy pieces must suggest the possibility of French manufacture, a theory confirmed, to some extent, by the quality of the metal and the general 'feel' of at least some of the pieces.* All examples so far attributed to this Group have decorative lines on the body as described on page 40.

Appendix II summarises, in tabular form for easy reference and identification, the distinctive characteristics of the four Groups of Jersey lidded flagons; statistical details of individual pieces in each Group are set out in Appendix I.

Fig. 14 Normandy jug—a type found with a hinge pin boss of Jersey Group 4 pattern.

*It is perhaps relevant to record that examples of Groups 1, 2 and 3 flagons tested, darkened immediately when treated with dilute nitric acid whereas Group 4 pieces and Normandy pieces with the 'dahlia' boss were hardly affected.

To set a date range for Guernsey flagons of Type I it will be necessary to mention briefly certain pewterers whose lives and work will be dealt with more fully in a later chapter. There are three recorded makers of this Type whose touches are struck on the London touch-plates and whose dates of qualification are known, namely: Joseph Wingod, James Tysoe and William de Jersey. A number of pieces by the first of these have been found and examined but, so far, none by either of the latter two makers has actually been seen by the authors and their identification with Guernsey flagons rests solely on Sutherland Graeme's findings.

Joseph Wingod became a Yeoman in 1721 and struck his touch in London in 1723: he is known to have been still alive in 1776, but by then must have been at least 79 years old; probably well beyond the age of active pewtering! It therefore seems reasonable to suggest 1725 to 1770 as being the most likely date range for his pieces. Joseph Wingod's son, John, was also a pewterer, but it is unlikely that he made any of the Guernsey pieces which bear his father's touch (even after the latter's retirement or death), as he had a recorded touch of his own, differing entirely from his father's, which he would surely have used: in any case, we know that he was bankrupt in 1767 and did not long outlive his father. John had a son, Cassia, also a pewterer (free in 1771 according to Cotterell), but there is no evidence that he was ever involved with the production of Channel Islands pewter, or, indeed, of any other. James Tysoe qualified as a pewterer in 1731 and died in 1774, whilst William de Jersey's dates are 1738 and 1785 respectively. Thus, their pieces, too, could embrace approximately the same period as Wingod's, though de Jersey could have continued a little longer – if indeed he ever made Guernsey flagons at all!

There is, however, an earlier maker, of whom brief mention has already been made, whose touch appears on one of the Guernsey type Seigneurial flagons of Sark. -IO:INGI.. can be seen above a date of 170?, with clasped hands below, in the touch, which is struck on top of the lid. A similar touch, with a clear date of 1706, found on a 9″ diameter plate, was noted by Cotterell after publication of *Old Pewter*, and two examples of the same mark have been found by the authors in Jersey, the first on an 8¼″ diameter multiple-reeded plate and the second, a very good striking, in the base of an English flat-lidded flagon (see Plate LV). Despite the doubt about the first letter or letters of the Christian name, it seems that this touch can only be that of Thomas Ingles, who qualified in 1706\07: no other 'INGLES' of suitable date has been recorded.

On the lid of the Sark piece are stamped the initials E L P, undoubtedly referring to a member of the Le Pelley family – an old and notable Island family, who bought the Seigneurie in 1730 – and, almost certainly, to one Elizabeth Le Pelley, of whom there were two in the 17th and 18th centuries. There were no male members of the family with Christian names beginning with E until well into the 19th century.

The first Elizabeth was born in 1641 and was married to one Jean Le Gros, who died in 1677: thereafter, as was customary, she reverted to her maiden name. Much of her subsequent life was spent in fighting a law case on behalf of her son against the de Carteret Seigneur, who was absent much of the time on his estates in Jersey: there is no doubt that she was an influential figure in the life of the Island. She died in 1726, by which time Ingles, based on his London 'freedom' in 1706, would probably have been just over 40. The second Elizabeth was the widow of Daniel Le Pelley, Seigneur of the Island, who died in 1752. For three years from that date she acted as Dame during the minority of her son. At this latter time Ingles would have been about 67, so that, purely chronologically, either identification is just about possible.

However, although the Sark flagon, which is a quart with a twin-bud thumbpiece, has generally similar characteristics to the pieces of Wingod and A. Carter (see below), it is somewhat cruder in form and has a handle directly attached to the body, without a stand-off strut; this is one of the features we have already noted in the earliest group of Jersey flagons and quite rare, also, amongst Guernseys. A second quart, with an apparently identical and very unusual LONDON stamp visible (see Plate LV), but with no signs of a touch remaining, is in the possession of one of the co-authors and a third similar piece has also been examined. These latter pieces also are without handle struts, are of similar 'early' form and are probably by the same maker, (whose touch has also been found on one pint flagon). In the light of these features it seems more probable that the initials E L P on the Sark flagon refer to the first Elizabeth Le Pelley and, if so, that it was made before her death in 1726, as it is hardly conceivable that such a utilitarian vessel would have been made or used commemoratively. This piece and its companions would therefore appear to represent some of the earliest Guernseys so far found. Perhaps ultimately, as in Jersey, evidence of still earlier examples will be discovered. One point of especial interest in regard to the Sark flagon is that it has stamped on it the official Guernsey verification seals of the rose and the fleur-de-lys – the only example of a normal Type I flagon yet found with these seals. As already stated, pewter measures were forbidden in Guernsey, but Sark was, and still is a law unto itself in such matters, though it falls, in some respects, within the territorial jurisdiction of Guernsey.

By far the greatest number of Type I Guernsey pieces – about 60% – are those which have been struck, on top of the lid, usually twice, with the 'Arms' mark containing the motto 'A POSSE AD ESSE'. These pieces are attributed by Cotterell to one A. Carter, c. 1750, and the Arms are certainly those of a branch of the Carter family (see Chapter dealing with the pewterers). These Arms are found on both plates and flagons; on the former accompanied by one or the other of the sets of initials CM or SM, struck within different incuse shapes, or by the full name 'A.CARTER' in a rectangle (see Plate LII). Flagons, however, have so far been found only with one or another of the three pairs of initials AC, CM, or SM and not with the full name of Carter. All these pieces bear a London 'label', which, on examples by AC and SM has the two letters 'N' reversed, thus 'LO ИD O И'; (so far only one exception to this rule, a flagon by SM, has been found with LONDON correctly spelled). Cotterell records the initialled marks of AC and SM but not that of CM: these CM pieces are, in fact, relatively scarce, comprising only about 10% of the 'Arms' flagons, in comparison with 55% in the case of SM and 35% for AC. Although all the pieces have a close family resemblance, those by CM seem generally better finished and the marks (other than the 'Arms' which are almost invariably weak) are well struck and from good dies. A variation of one of the main Guernsey characteristics is not infrequently found in this Group – namely, the substitution of a series of incised lines for the more usual decoration of three raised bands around the belly of the flagon. These lines have so far been found on pieces bearing the marks SM and CM and not on those with AC.

Suggestions as to the names of the owners of these initials will be put forward later: for the purposes of this Chapter we need note only that their pieces bear very close resemblance indeed to the general characteristics, style and manufacture of the Wingod pieces, as well as to their usual condition and general appearance of age. It is our opinion, confirmed by the rim type of plates with the same touches, that this large group also falls within the Wingod period, i.e. 1725 to 1770, and the circa 1750 as suggested by Cotterell (for AC) is a reasonable central point pending more precise dating in the light of new information.

We have yet to mention flagons with touches bearing the initialled marks of TC (Cott. 5530) (Plate LII) and PSH (unrecorded) (Plate LVII), each of which have been found struck on top of the lid, and AD, relief cast, *inside* the lid (also unrecorded) (see Plate LII). In Chapter 6 we have hazarded a mere guess at a possible name for the pewterer with the initials TC. If our guess is correct then these flagons would be earlier than the general run of Guernseys and probably contemporaneous with those of Ingles. One of the pieces found with this touch has a handle fixed directly to the body without a strut (apparently its original form), and this could be regarded as offering some evidence of this chronology.

Only one flagon, a pint with twin-acorn thumbpiece (see Plate XII), has been found with the touch PSH. We have no evidence at all of the identity of this pewterer and can hope only that future research will

XII Guernsey pint flagon of unusual form, maker PSH; possibly late 18th century.

reveal his name and provenance. The flagon appears to be late in date and indeed the skirt and lid have very much the character of those of Type II. There are, however, the usual Type I decorative raised bands around the neck and a series of incised lines around the belly, similar to some of the pieces with the touches CM and SM.

Four pieces only, three pints and one half-pint, have been found with the initials AD relief cast *inside* the lid. Again, unfortunately, we can offer no suggestions as to the maker's identity. The pieces appear 'early', i.e. possibly before 1725, and have the handle attached directly to the body. The general form is similar to other flagons of Type I, but there are differences in detail (see Chapter 5).

We have suggested a latest date of about 1770 for the Guernsey Type I and of *c.* 1765 for the Jersey flagons of Group 3, the largest of the Jersey Groups. This (though perhaps a little earlier) tallies fairly closely with the time that the production of lidded flagons and measures began to decrease in England. It is possible that other pewterers continued to use existing moulds after the known makers retired, or, alternatively, that some of them may have continued to work to a later date than we have assumed. However, we have found no evidence of this at all and in the light of present knowledge, therefore, we would maintain the dates already suggested for these types.

Group 4 Jerseys and Type II Guernseys, however, are a different matter. As to the former we have already suggested that they belong to an appreciably later period – a revival, perhaps brought about by a particular need for new lidded flagons to replace or supplement those last made many years before.

Type II Guernseys could have arisen from a similar need. These pieces have their lids deeply and crisply stamped on top* with the initials Ns L Ct, flanked by two Tudor roses and with GUERNESEY (sic) below – the old French spelling but still used on coinage until after the Second World War (see Plate LVI). These flagons are frequently in a very good to immaculate state of preservation and often show evidence of considerable machine manufacture or finishing: many, too, have the Guernsey verification seals of rose and fleur-de-lys on the lip, unknown on standard skirted Type I Guernseys except for the Sark example for which a special explanation can be adduced. Although some are well made and heavy, others are somewhat crude both in form and manufacture and are light and thin, especially the lid; generally, however, the appearance and 'feel' of all of these pieces suggest that they are much later than Type I. The owner of the initials Ns L Ct has so far not been traced, nor do we know for certain whether he was a maker or a dealer, though much more likely the latter for reasons explained in Chapter 5. An exact dating, therefore, has not been possible, but the visual evidence suggests that

XIII Mould of 13 sections (belonging to The Pewter Society) for a Channel Islands pint flagon, with a piece cast from it.

they are certainly not earlier than about 1780 extending perhaps to *c.* 1830 and possibly even later. Two of the unmarked specimens (see footnote p. 49) have been found engraved with initials and dates of 1793 and 1797, no doubt marking some special occasions. As new vessels would almost certainly have been used for such a purpose, these pieces provide some evidence of the validity of our general assumption about this Type.

Where these Guernsey Type II pieces came from is again a somewhat open question. In view of the shape, previous Jersey moulds – perhaps even those of de St. Croix – may have been used, suitably adapted at the foot, or new moulds made from a Jersey pattern. It is, however, considered most unlikely that these pieces were actually manufactured in Jersey for the reasons that (a), the probable time span is well documented and no evidence of any kind has been found of pewter manufacture in the Island at the time; (b), very few pieces of this Type have been found in the Island and, except for the unmarked examples, most are known to have been brought from Guernsey relatively recently, and (c), there is no tradition of one Island making for export to the other in any phase of commerce or industry.

It seems equally unlikely that they were made in Guernsey. In that Island, too, the period is well documented and no pewterer at all has been traced. Furthermore, as we have already pointed out, some unmarked pieces, clearly from the same moulds though made to Jersey capacities, have been found in Jersey, so in this case, too, reason (c) mentioned in the preceding paragraph would apply – in any case why no maker's (or factor's) initial stamp on the lid even though the Island name were omitted?

This appears to leave only England, or perhaps France, as possible alternatives. We do not favour the latter for a variety of reasons and the metal, style and general 'feel' of the majority of these pieces seem to have little resemblance to the French pewter of the period. On the other hand, the metal and manufacture have something in common with English tavernware of the period, perhaps provincially made, for example in the West Country. On balance, therefore, we incline to the view that both the marked and the unmarked Type II pieces were made in England, the majority being exported to Guernsey and stamped by Ns L Ct, either before shipment or after arrival in that Island, and the unmarked pieces being shipped direct to Jersey, perhaps not even passing through the hands of Ns L Ct. This theory, and other matters relating to the possible identity and location of Ns L Ct, will be discussed further in Chapter 6.

It is appropriate here to mention a flagon-mould bequeathed to The Pewter Society (of England) by the late Mr. R. W. Cooper. It consists of 13 sections (see Plate XIII), very well made in gunmetal (good quality bronze). Plate XIV shows a flagon cast from this mould and, as will be seen by comparison with the pieces illustrated in Plate XL, it resembles very closely indeed the shape of the Guernsey Type II flagons (both the marked and the unmarked varieties). The only visible differences are in the size of the lid, the form of the wedge (which is rather more like the Guernsey Type I) and the position of the lower end of the handle, which is somewhat 'higher' up the body. The first two points could be simply accounted for by the use of a different lid and thumbpiece section (with this mould the lid, wedge and thumbpiece are cast integrally) – a by no means unlikely possibility in view of the appreciable variations in manufacture of Type II pieces to which we have already referred. The third point, the position of the lower end of the handle, is also susceptible of a fairly simple explanation viz: the capacity of the piece cast from this mould is 611 ccs, some 10% greater than the equivalent Type II capacity: however, the piece is also about 12 mm taller than the equivalent Type II. If the lip were cut down by this amount not only would the capacity of the piece seem likely to be very close to the Type II standard, but also the handle would be lowered with the result that the bottom fixing would be in just about the same position as it is on the Type II pieces. In all the circumstances, therefore, we consider this to be a mould for Type II 'Guernsey' flagons.

As in the case of Jersey flagons, an identification chart has been prepared (Appendix IV) tabulating marks, characteristics, possible dates and other information relating to Guernsey vessels: statistical details of individual pieces are set out in Appendix III.

XIV Pint flagon cast from mould shown in Plate XIII.

3

Unlidded Measures

We now turn our attention to unlidded vessels: these are designated as 'measures' for the simple reason that between 85% and 90% of those examined have had verification seals stamped on the lip and this was required only on vessels used or intended primarily to be used, for measuring. Moreover the large majority, about 80%, are found in the smaller sizes of pint, half-pint and noggin, sizes which would be of very limited use for the staple tipples of cider, wine or beer.

Although the term 'Channel Islands' is often applied to these pieces, in fact, despite the different forms found, all are variants of the basic Jersey pattern. Their general shape has little or no similarity to the normal Guernsey Type I; they lack any of its typical banded decoration and, although an occasional specimen has a pronounced foot rim or base moulding, it is quite different from the Guernsey skirt. Nevertheless, although probably produced for the Jersey market, and used primarily in that Island where pewter measures had always been permitted, it is clear that some were imported into Guernsey and used there also. This is evidenced by the Guernsey verification seals of the rose and the fleur-de-lys found on a small number of examples *of Type (b)* only.*

One interesting fact is that no example has been found with both Jersey and Guernsey seals, which might suggest direct export to each Island from the source of supply. The acceptance of these pieces for stamping in Guernsey presumably would have taken place after the strict prohibition on the use of pewter measures in that Island had fallen into desuetude – a situation we have already noted as apparently having occurred in the case of Type II Guernsey lidded flagons.

It had previously been accepted that only five sizes of unlidded measures existed, from quart down to half noggin. However, we have found a unique example, of pot size, of the blind hinge boss variety (see below), and must accept the possibility that others exist.† Nevertheless, it should here be stated that Channel Islands unlidded measures are relatively scarce in all sizes – certainly scarcer than the larger sizes of the lidded flagons.

---

*see Page 53 for description of types of unlidded measures.

---

*We have also found two pieces with an 'intermediate' capacity of 1½ pints (on the Jersey standard).

There are several varieties of unlidded measures with both major and minor differences in body shape, handle, base, decoration, etc. We have, however, endeavoured to group them, firstly, by the form and fixing of the handle, and, secondly, by certain general features, particularly the foot rim.

There are three main variations of handle shape:
(a) those with an unpierced hinge boss at the top (see Fig. 15),
(b1) those with a continuous sweep from the lip to the belly, but with a thickening at the top fixture point (see Fig. 16) and
(b2) those with a small 'step' close to the junction with the lip but otherwise closely similar to (b) (see Fig. 17). Although (b1) and (b2) are mentioned as separate varieties in fact the difference does not appear to be important. Frequently the 'step' is minimal or merely indicated by a thickening of the metal and on some examples it is not easy to be sure that there has not been a subsequent distortion which has altered the form of the handle. As there are no significant variations in other features, therefore, it will be convenient to consider (b1) and (b2) simply as one Type (b).

On both Types, (a) and (b),* the bottom of the handle is finished with a slightly rounded end just below the point of fixing but Type (a) appears always to have the handle affixed directly to the body of the measure whilst Type (b) has a small stand-off strut (see Figs. 16 and 17), similar to

Handle

Fig. 15 Handle of Type (a) unlidded measures.

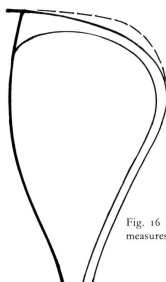

Fig. 16 Handle of Type (b1) unlidded measures.

Fig. 17 Handle of Type (b2) unlidded measures.

*Hereafter the Terms 'Type (a)' and 'Type (b)' are used to denote the measure as a whole and not merely the form of its handle.

the majority of the lidded flagons. There is usually a perceptible difference between the two Types in regard to the general shape and angle of the handle: Type (a) generally has a fairly straight, or only slightly curved, main section whilst Type (b) is frequently much more curved (compare Figs. 15 and 16). Also whilst both Types have rather strap-like handles, those of Type (b) are generally narrower and somewhat cruder. Slight variations occur at the top of the Type (b) handle: in some examples it springs horizontally from the lip for a short distance (about half an inch or so, depending on the size of the measure, or to the step if there is one) whereas in other cases it slopes straight downwards from the lip sometimes at quite a steep angle. These differences often appear to be original and not due to subsequent damage or stress (see dotted and solid lines in Figs. 16 and 17).

Occasionally handles are found which do not conform to either of the foregoing Types. We have noted examples with more than one 'step' at the top, some with a concave section or upward slope immediately adjoining the lip (see Fig. 18(a) and (b)), and still others with a small curved terminal at the base of the handle, (see Fig. 19). All such handles so far found have been fixed directly to the body without a stand-off strut. Generally the shape of these handles is much more curved than the other Types (see Fig. 18(b)) and the handle itself is often thicker, rounder or 'D' shaped in section and not strap-like. For ease of reference, measures showing any of these variations are grouped together as 'Type (c)'.

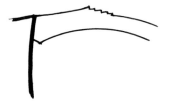

Fig. 18 a. and b. Handles of Type (c) unlidded measures.

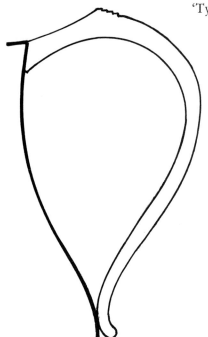

Fig. 19 Extended terminal–Type (c) unlidded measures.

Shapes of unlidded measures seem to vary appreciably, ranging from those with a very incurved neck swelling out into a well rounded belly similar to the lidded flagons, to those with a 'slim' form throughout resembling an early English baluster (see Plates XV, LXII, LXIII and LXIV). Measures of Type (a), i.e. with the unpierced hinge boss, are normally of the former pattern, but Types (b) and (c) come in all shapes, though the pint and half-pint are generally the more bulbous: no Type (b) or (c) pots or quarts have been found. All unlidded measures of Types (a) and (c) seem to have a completely circular top without a 'pinched' spout for pouring, but Type (b) measures are sometimes found with this spout.

Shape and General Features

XV

a. Group of Type (a) unlidded measures (with blind hinge boss).

b. Group of Type (b) unlidded measures with handle and foot variations.

55

Fig. 20 Base forms of unlidded measures.

The most interesting variations occur at the foot where four main forms have been noted (see Fig. 20):

(i) with a very slight outward curve below the belly,

(ii) similar to (i) but finished at the base with a small ovolo moulding with an incised line at its top,

(iii) with a much more pronounced eversion, usually with the ovolo moulding as in (ii), and similar to the general shape of the lidded flagons,

(iv) with either a complete and fairly deep, incurved, decorative base moulding, or, alternatively, form (iii) with an additional raised or incised line or lines at the top of the eversion.

Type (a), with the unpierced hinge boss, appears to be the most consistent, being almost always accompanied by base (ii), or very occasionally base (i). Type (b) may be found with any one of the foot varieties, but most often with bases (ii) and (iii): measures of Type (c) tend to have a fairly plain base such as (i) or (ii).

Decoration, other than the rather exceptional foot moulding of base (iv), is limited to incised lines, usually around the lip, near the bottom of the neck, below the belly and at or above the foot mould. The lines are usually in pairs close together, except for the single one forming the top of the ovolo foot moulding. One rather unusual noggin (see Plate XVI) has three deep grooves around the body just above mid-height producing an effect somewhat similar to the decorative treatment on the Falaise flagon shown in Plate IV. Types (a) and (c) unlidded measures generally have no decoration at all other than the foot ovolo, but a high percentage of Type (b) have incised lines around one or more sections of the body, though not, apparently, to any consistent grouping. To summarise we suggest the following as the most usual group features of unlidded measures:

Type (a) – With unpierced hinge boss, a strap-like handle with a fairly straight main section, fixed direct to the body without a stand-off strut. The body is generally more bulbous, with a short everted section under the belly, finished with a small ovolo base moulding with a single incised line at its top. No other decoration on the body. Found in six sizes, but the pot is, so far, unique.

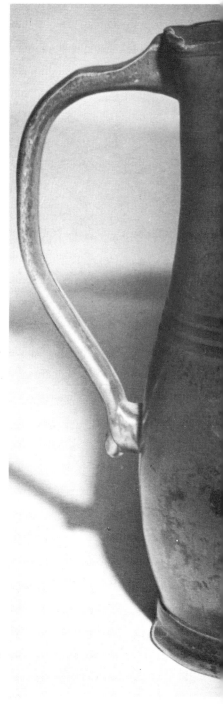

XVI Unusual unlidded measure of noggin size (see Page 65).

56

Type (b) – Handle, usually strap-like, either in a continuous sweep from lip to body or 'stepped' near the lip; sometimes springing horizontally from the lip and sometimes angled down, but in either case fixed to the body at its lower end by a short stand-off strut. So far found only in the sizes of pint, half-pint, noggin and half-noggin. The body sometimes bulbous in the two larger sizes, but generally 'slim'. The base with or without moulding, and the body frequently decorated with incised lines.

Type (c) – Several different forms of handle, but generally more curved than Types (a) and (b) and with several 'steps'. The handle itself rounded, or 'D' shaped, in section rather than strap-like, and fixed direct to the body at the lower end. Generally no decoration except a base moulding. Normally found only in the sizes of pint, half-pint and noggin, but one example has been found of a one and a half pint size.

Types (a) and (b) occur in almost equal proportions, each accounting for at least 45% of all the unlidded measures found, with the remaining 10% or less belonging to Type (c). Examples of all Types appear in Plates LXII, LXIII and LXIV.

Capacities of all Types seem to be generally similar to those of the lidded Jersey flagons, and these will be discussed fully in a later chapter, together with verification seals, which are also found in identical form on both lidded and unlidded vessels, though much more frequently on the unlidded. Owner's initials, generally in the typical Channel Islands form, are found on many unlidded measures, usually crudely scratched on the handle, as in the case of the lidded flagons. Occasionally, however, they may be found engraved or stamped on the body or on the base of the measure and a very few examples have been found with a full name engraved round the body in a style similar to that used on early 19th century English public house ware.

We have now to consider when these measures were made, and where. It was tempting to assume that those of Type (a) with the blind hinge boss were the earliest and that they were made from the same moulds used for the Jersey Group 3 lidded flagons, either after these ceased to be made around 1765 or even contemporaneously with them. There are, however, certain pointers which suggest that this assumption in regard to relative dating may not be correct. Firstly the handle of this Type is always affixed directly to the body without a stand-off strut; secondly the shape, although very similar to the lidded variety, is not absolutely identical, especially at the foot, and even the hinge boss itself is slightly different, being often too far from the body to carry a hinge spindle; thirdly many of this Type are found in unexpectedly good condition, and fourthly the general style is clean-cut and sophisticated and some

XVII Mark of 'open left hand' with cross in palm, found in the base of some unlidded measures – actual size, finger tip to wrist, 5 mm. This mark has also been found on English tavernware of the early part of the 19th century. Note rather unusual form of Crown over 'X' alongside.
(Photo: Senett & Spears, Jersey).

examples show evidence of appreciable machine finishing. The first point, in particular, seems to require explanation since there appears to be no valid reason for omitting the strut on an unlidded measure made at the same time as, or immediately following the strutted lidded pieces and perhaps from the same moulds.

Nothing resembling a maker's touch has been found on any measures of this Type except for an open left hand (with a cross in the palm), and a crowned 'X' alongside (see Plate XVII), struck in the bottom of the unique hinge boss pot. This mark has been identified as having been used by Gaskell, either alone or in partnership, and has been found identically on certain pieces of English tavernware, which could be dated 10 years or so either side of 1830, as well as on two small spirit measures mentioned later in this chapter. Verification seals provide little positive help in dating, except to show that the majority of unlidded measures were in use sometime in Queen Victoria's reign or earlier (see Chapter 4). We must, therefore, consider other evidence. Firstly, as it is clear that the lidded flagons were used to some extent as measures – as evidenced by verification seals – there would seem to have been little need for the manufacture of the unlidded types whilst the former were still in production, and this would be very much in conformity with what happened in the United Kingdom. Secondly, the existence of so many of the smaller sizes of the unlidded measures suggests that they were used for a more potent liquor than the staple drinks of milk, cider, beer or wine – a noggin of any of these would have done little to satisfy a thirsty agricultural worker – and, although clearly one cannot dogmatise, the more general consumption of 'strong' liquors in the Islands seems to have occurred in the 19th rather than in the 18th century. Thirdly, it is fair to consider the visual evidence of the pieces themselves – their apparent age, form of manufacture, type of metal and general 'feel'.

In the light of all the foregoing factors we would be inclined to suggest a date for Type (a) measures beginning not much earlier than 1800, and extending to, at least, 1840 but possibly even later.

As to where they were made, it seems very possible that at least some parts of existing Jersey type moulds were used and, therefore, manufacture of these unlidded vessels either in Jersey itself or in England might seem most likely, though, in the light of our comments on the Group 4 lidded flagons, we must not overlook the bare possibility of French manufacture: the metal and general style, however, seem quite different from those of the Group 4 pieces. We have found no evidence whatsoever for Jersey manufacture despite the fairly good documentation of this period, though it is just possible that the de St. Croix moulds may have been in the Island, as they have been reported to have been at a later date.

As far as we are aware, very few English measures with the blind hinge boss were made, though some Scottish pieces are known. Nevertheless the manufacture, quality of metal and finish are usually very good, and, on balance, we must consider that these pieces were made in the United Kingdom as part of the large output of tavern pewter produced at this time. An apparent problem of capacity might be mentioned: Jersey measures, as we shall see in a later chapter, conformed neither to the Old English Ale or Wine Standards in general use before 1826, nor to Imperial measure used thereafter. However any difficulties of special production would have been self-correcting if existing Jersey moulds were basically used.

We turn now to measures of Type (b). Although there are several varieties of measures of this Type, the date range would appear to be fairly consistent. None of these pieces bear any maker's marks. Verification seals are of types similar to those found on the lidded measures and, in themselves, give little indication of dating beyond the fact that they show that the measures were certainly in use during the 19th century (see Chapter 4).

Contrary to initial supposition, these measures do, in fact, appear *visually* to be older than Type (a). They also have the handle fixed to the body through a small stand-off strut and this could substantiate a slightly earlier dating than the blind boss measures which have the handle connected directly to the body. It could be that these measures follow on fairly soon after Group 3 lidded flagons ceased to be made – in about 1765, if our previous assumptions are correct. The general appearance, feel and metal of most of these pieces, and the way in which they have aged, are all very reminiscent of the tavern pewter made and used in England towards the end of the 18th century and during the first decades of the 19th.* Without any more definite evidence on which to base an opinion, therefore, we are inclined to the view that the majority of Jersey measures of this Type were made in England, specifically for the Channel Islands market, and possibly over a period from about 1780 to 1830. Some pieces, however, have a form of decoration (i.e. incised lines around the body in several places), type of metal and general 'feel' quite reminiscent of the Group 4 lidded flagons, and this is a subject which might justify further investigation, especially into the possibility of French manufacture.

Because of the kind of use to which these vessels were put in taverns and elsewhere, they probably did not last long and were repeatedly being replaced; thus, the bulk of the earliest pieces are no longer extant. We are, however, aware that fairly recent research in the United Kingdom has suggested that unlidded measures and tankards generally may be appreciably earlier than had been thought previously, having perhaps been made, even in some quantity, quite early in the 18th century. It may be that a similar state of affairs existed in regard to Jersey pewter and that some, at least, of the extant pieces in one, or both, of the preceding Types may be earlier than we have credited.

Type (c) measures appear to comprise a relatively small group. All the examples of this Type that we have so far examined have had the handle fixed directly to the body at the lower end; most, too, seem to show appreciable evidence of machine operations and are generally in very good condition with edges still sharp. Again these pieces have no marks, other than verification seals which merely indicate use at least during the 19th century, but the visual evidence, including the shape of the handle, suggests that the majority are later than Types (a) and (b) – possibly substantially so. Generally we are inclined to date these pieces from the middle of the 19th century extending, perhaps, almost to 1900.

Although the foregoing types cover all the unlidded measures of traditional Jersey baluster shape which have so far come to light, there are other forms of measures which have been used in Jersey, as evidenced by the verification seals found on them, and which must, therefore, be considered. The most interesting of these is the conical shaped, spouted can of which two examples are shown in Plate XVIII.

*Capacities, except in rare cases, conform quite closely to the Jersey standards (see Chapter 4), and not to the English.

xviii Two Jersey conical 'can' measures of quart and pint capacity (see Page 71).

This shape, *made in copper or brass*, was widely used in the Island, certainly during late Victorian times and perhaps even earlier. Measures like these were used by merchants selling wine and cider, or hard liquor such as gin and brandy, by retail from the casks in their warehouses, measuring the required quantity into jugs or other receptacles brought by their customers. A similar shape seems also to have been used for paraffin and other oils. Many of the older inhabitants of the Island remember the shape well, but none that we have yet asked can recall having previously seen one made in pewter. Nevertheless, two examples have been found and are in the writer's collection; they are a pint and a quart, identical in shape and form although purchased from quite different sources. They are struck with capacity Seal 'B' (see Chapter 4), and are of 'Jersey' capacity, being of 525 ccs and 1045 ccs respectively – very close indeed to both the theoretical and empirical Jersey standards (see Chapter 4), and far removed from Imperial or the Old English Standards.

The handles are typical of English early 19th century tankards, being 'stepped' at the top, hollow and 'D' shaped in section and fixed direct to the body at the lower end. In default of any more conclusive evidence,

61

XIX English tavern measures with Jersey verification seals.

and in the light of their general appearance, we would assume that they were made in England for use in Jersey between about 1800 and 1840. We shall be most interested to see whether the publication of this information reveals other sizes in this pattern – perhaps a whole range of six sizes were made as in other forms.

English tavern measures and tankards of the early 19th century form the second group of non-traditional Island shape on which Jersey capacity seals are found. Quite a number of examples, both of the cylindrical and bulbous types (see Plate XIX), have been found so sealed. Although a few are of pre-Imperial capacities, the majority are of the Imperial standard in various sizes from a quart downwards. Most of these pieces are stamped with Seal 'B' (see Chapter 4), which indicates use at least in the Victorian period (and in some cases perhaps even earlier), and some have, in addition, seals relating to the 20th century.

The fact that Imperial capacity pieces have been found so sealed should in no way be taken as indicating that Imperial was an official standard in the Island – it was not until January 1st 1919. The explanation is, almost certainly, that the controls relating to capacity verification were not always very strictly administered in the Island and that, provided the vessel complied with at least the minimum 'Jersey' standard, it would be

xx Unusual French lidless measure with Jersey verification seal and of 1½ pints (Jersey) capacity.

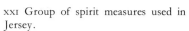

xxi Group of spirit measures used in Jersey.

sealed, apparently almost irrespective of its excess capacity.

Perhaps not unexpectedly, we have also found a few French vessels, both lidded and unlidded, stamped with Jersey verification seals, usually that relating to the period 1754–1901 (see Fig. 22). In every case these pieces have complied with the minimum 'Jersey' standard. One unusual unlidded specimen of Normandy origin (see Plate xx) had a capacity of one and a half Jersey pints, as in the case of the Type (c) Jersey measure referred to on Page 57.

Finally we should mention that, occasionally, small pewter spirit measures are found, of a fairly typical English, cylindrical, tapering form (see Plate xxi) stamped either with the Jersey verification seal which relates to the 19th century (or earlier), or with the word 'JERSEY'. Examples both of local (Jersey) and of Imperial Standard have been recorded. Measures of this type were at one time not uncommon in public houses, but all now seem to have been replaced by vessels of somewhat similar shape in other metals or in glass. Two of the examples found had the mark of an open left hand stamped in the bottom of the measure, apparently identical to the mark found inside the unique blind hinge boss measure of pot size referred to on page 56 (see Plate xvii).

Capacities and verification seals will be discussed in the next chapter.

4 Capacities and Verification Seals

Because of the close links between the Channel Islands and France, it could be expected that the capacities and sizes of pewter flagons and measures and the names associated with them would, quite clearly, be based on one or other of the French systems and most probably on one of the many that existed in Normandy. In fact, as will emerge, some aspects of the subject have been found to be both confused and complex. Nevertheless a large body of information has been gathered from relevant Laws and Reports of the Islands' States and Courts, and from other documents that have been discovered. The contents of this chapter and the conclusions we have drawn will, we hope, to some extent clarify the position; they are the results not only of the information so gathered, but also, as in the case of most other facets of Channel Islands pewter, of the close examination and measurement of a large number of flagons and measures and a personal interpretation of the factual data so obtained.

Jersey Capacities   As far as Jersey is concerned there are six basic sizes of flagons or measures* and the names applied to these sizes, in descending order of capacity, are as follows: pot (pronounced 'po' locally as in French), quart, pint, half-pint, noggin and half-noggin.† The reasons for the selection of these names will appear later, but the pot, quart(e), and noggin (or noguin) are specifically mentioned in enactments of the 17th and 18th centuries, thus covering the earliest significant period in relation to extant Jersey pewter. It should perhaps be made clear at the outset that the local Jersey capacities that we shall be studying were quite different from those in use in the United Kingdom and that, therefore, where terms such as 'quart' and 'pint' are used they do not indicate the same capacities as those to which these names are, or were, applied in England.

The basic capacity standard referred to in old Jersey documents and used 'from time immemorial' is the CABOT, applied to both dry and liquid measure and derived from French, and most probably Normandy sources as in the case of the weights used in the Island. (As far back as

*but see preceding chapter regarding two examples of an extra 'intermediate' size (of one and a half 'Jersey' pints).

the 16th century the ancient Marc (or standard) of Rouen was officially declared to be the legal weight for the Island and has been so until the present century, the Jersey pound avoirdupois of 16 ounces equalling 7561 grains Imperial). However, prior to the introduction of the metric system into France, there was a very wide range of local capacity measures, even in a relatively small area such as Normandy, and it has not been possible to trace definitively the exact origin of the Jersey Cabot.

Nevertheless the opinion of such an authority as R. R. Lempriere, Viscount of Jersey during the late Victorian period and the early years of this century, must be seriously considered. He was the Crown official responsible for checking local weights and measures and made a close study of them and of their history. In a memorandum on the subject, dated 1914, he pointed out that the 'pot d'Arques' was the base of all measures of capacity in the Department of the Seine-Inferieure in France, and that $10\frac{3}{4}$ of these pots equalled a 'Bushel of "Eu"'. He then stated 'I take this "Bushel of 'Eu'" to be the same as the Cabot of Jersey'. No evidence has been found to challenge this opinion – indeed quite the contrary – though perhaps it should be mentioned that Eu is some 50 miles away from Rouen, where the Jersey weight system originated.

A standard cabot measure still exists in Jersey (see Plate XXII). It is an unlidded brass vessel of respectable antiquity – certainly early 18th century and probably much earlier – and all the evidence suggests that this is the actual vessel referred to as the Standard in legal and other documents over the centuries. It has a diameter of $14\frac{7}{8}''$ at the top and is $8\frac{1}{2}''$ high and it contains (according to measurements made by Messrs. Avery & Sons of London in 1912), 304,288 grains, or 19,718 cubic centimetres of water. The latter is a more convenient and appropriate standard of measurement, especially with the imminent British change to the metric system, and will henceforth be used throughout this work. The capacity of this vessel compares very closely indeed with that of the Bushel of 'Eu', the difference being only just over $\frac{1}{2}\%$,* a quite acceptable variation in the light of the probable standards of accuracy of measurement and manufacture at the time and clearly favouring Lempriere's opinion of the derivation of the Jersey Cabot.

This Cabot was originally known as the 'estendard du Château' (standard of the Castle), the title having probably derived from the fact that in former times the measure was kept in Mont Orgueil Castle at Gorey in the east of the Island. However, a vessel of this magnitude (nearly $4\frac{1}{2}$ gallons) was clearly not a practical standard for the verification of flagons of a size likely to be used on farms, or in inns and shops for the measurement or sale of wine, cider, beer and (probably later) spirits. Indeed it is known that it was not so used since two other capacity standards are specifically referred to in the laws covering the period; these

†Gill Wylie, in *Pewter, Measure for Measure*, illustrates a range of *seven* pieces, which he attributes to Jersey, the smallest size being a quarter-noggin. However, having received, through the courtesy of Mr. William O. Blaney of the Pewter Collectors Club of America, a photographic enlargement of the latter piece, we believe it to be of French, and not of Channel Islands, origin. Although the body shape is not dissimilar to that of some Jersey flagons, especially perhaps those of Group 4 (for which we have already adumbrated a possible French origin!), it has a pronounced collar around the top not found on the Jersey pattern, though common on many types of French pichets. The handle, too, resembles the French shape rather than the Jersey and, although it is never easy to be certain from a photograph alone, the piece does not have a Channel Islands 'feel' at all.

*Based on the figures quoted by Lempriere for the Pot d'Arques, the Bushel of "Eu" contained 19,608 cubic centimetres.

XXII The standard Jersey 'Cabot' (measure of capacity), made of brass; height 216mm., top diameter 376mm. (In the possession of the Department of Weights & Measures, Jersey).

are the pot and the quart. As early as 1617, in an Act of the Jersey Court, the 'estendard du Château' is decreed as the Island's basic legal standard of capacity, and this Act refers still further back to the 'orders of the Royal Commissioners' of 1562. Subsequently in 1625 the Court affirms that the pot is to be one tenth of the 'estendard du Chateau' and the quart one twentieth.

It was, however, the quart that ultimately became the actual liquid capacity standard, as determined by the Royal Court of Jersey in Regulations made in 1754, and subsequently codified in the Law of 1771, which states:

> '*A certain vessel of brass containing a quart* according to the Standard of the Castle, which contains 10 pots, and marked by the Viscount in conformity with the Regulations established by the Court of Heritage on the second day of May 1754, *shall serve as the standard of liquid measures.*'

The quart was thus an 'established size' in the 18th century when the majority of extant Jersey flagons and measures were being made.

The pot and the quart therefore form the basis of a hierarchy of sizes for flagons and measures. Our empirical measurements have established conclusively that the remaining four sizes found in the Jersey form were intended to be half the capacity of the next larger size.* It has therefore been considered appropriate to follow the quart with the 'pint' and 'half-pint', and for the two smaller sizes the terms 'noggin' and 'half-noggin' have been adopted, the former being found in local documents of the mid 18th century as 'noguin' (or Jersey-French 'Nodgîn').

---

*but see footnote to page 64 regarding two examples of an 'intermediate' size (of one and a half 'Jersey' pints).

The complete scale of Jersey measures is therefore as follows:
1 POT = 2 QUARTS = 4 PINTS = 8 HALF-PINTS = 16 NOGGINS = 32 HALF-NOGGINS.

It should perhaps be mentioned that, except in house inventories, we have found no documentary references to the terms 'pint' and 'half-pint' in Jersey prior to the 19th century, though they are mentioned in Guernsey as early as the beginning of the 17th century. The Island capacity nomenclature is, in fact, somewhat complex: the terms 'quarte' and 'pinte' were formerly used in France, though for varying capacities; 'pot', although very generally used in France, was also used in England in the 16th century for a measure of unknown size and 'pottle', also in England, as early as the 13th century* denoting a half-gallon sized measure, which is of the same order of size as the Jersey pot. The word 'noguin' or 'nodgin' does not appear in French (or in English in that form) and may be peculiar to Jersey.

As to the actual standards themselves, the volume of the Cabot has already been quoted, as measured by Messrs. Avery, at 19,718 cubic centimetres. The pot, therefore, being one tenth of the cabot according to the enactments of 1625, 1754 and 1771, should be 1,972 ccs and the quart thus 968 ccs.

However, in September 1827 the States of Jersey decided that the rules governing weights and measures in the Island were inadequate, as it had been discovered that many measures which should have been of the same size were, in fact, quite different; they therefore set up a Committee to examine the whole subject and to prepare a report. The actual report presented by this Committee has unfortunately not been traced, but it was considered by the States on January 12th 1828 and the minutes of that meeting were quite full and precise. The States noted that the quart measure referred to in the Law of 1771, which was to have served as the liquid capacity standard in the future 'no longer existed' but that, comparing the 'Standard of the Castle' (the cabot) with liquid measures stamped by the Viscount, which had been used 'in all antiquity', it had been found that the Cabot, instead of containing 10 pots, contained only 9 pots 2½ pints or 1½ pints (about 7%) less than the theoretical old standard of 10 pots.

After careful consideration and 'in order not to make any change in the ancient measures', the States decided:
(i) that the Cabot should henceforth be held to contain 9 pots 2½ pints,
(ii) that the Viscount should arrange to have made, in brass, a pot, a quart, a pint, a half-pint, a noggin and a half-noggin conforming to this new standard and
(iii) that he should retain these vessels for verifying all new measures.

On this new basis, but still working on Messrs. Avery's actual

*Vide "Libra" (Journal of the Weights and Measures History Circle), Vol. 2, No. 4, December 1963.

measurement of the Cabot of 19,718 ccs, the pot would be 2,049 ccs to the nearest cubic centimetre, the quart 1,024 ccs, the pint 512 ccs, the half-pint 256 ccs, the noggin 128 ccs and the half-noggin 64 ccs. Measures of copper, which appear to be of the right age to have been those ordered by the States in 1828, are, in fact, still in the possession of the Weights and Measures Department in Jersey for the sizes of pot, noggin and half-noggin (but not a quart, pint or half-pint). These three measures have been tested by the Department and have been found to contain 2074 ccs, 127½ ccs and 64 ccs of water respectively. It will be noted that the noggin and half-noggin conform exactly to the 'new' cabot standard of 1828 but the pot is 25 ccs (or about 1¼%) too large.

There is actually a presently existing quart standard also, but of a different shape, and of brass. It is a very well made vessel with the name of the makers, Messrs. De Grave, Short and Fenner of London thereon and the date 1845. This has a capacity (according to measurements also made by Messrs. Avery), of 1,045 ccs. It was made on the orders of the Viscount of the time, Col. Le Couteur, but on what basis is a mystery, since it does not conform either to the old 10 pot cabot standard (which gave a quart of 968 ccs) or to the new 1828 9 pot 2½ pint standard (which gave 1,024 ccs for the quart). It is especially strange that it is larger than either of these capacities because the Viscount records in his correspondence his strong disapproval of the States decision of 1828 to 'debase' the Cabot thereby causing loss of revenue to the Island.

From the foregoing paragraphs it might appear that the standards of measurement for liquids in Jersey were very uncertain and open to criticism. However the Island was by no means unique in this respect: in England, at times, more than one standard existed for the same 'size', and measurements carried out on English baluster measures* show great variations in capacity for apparently similar 'sizes'. On the other side of the Channel the situation was even worse. In Normandy, for example, every town of any size seems to have had its own, quite different, standard, and indeed the general situation was so bad that ultimately Necker, the French Finance Minister, advised Louis XVI that the whole state of measures throughout the country was in such chaos that the only thing to do was to scrap the lot and start again. The introduction of the metric system was the ultimate result.

To return to Jersey, it would appear that there are four possible bases of computation for the standard quart (and hence for the other sizes relatively), viz:

(a) on the Bushel of 'Eu', when it would be 980 ccs.

(b) on the Cabot of 10 pots making it 986 ccs.

(c) on the Cabot of 9 pots 2½ pints making it 1,024 ccs, and

(d) on the standard quart of 1845 itself, being 1,045 ccs.

*Dr. R.F.Homer, 1960/61, in *The Pewter Society Journal* (Reprinted March 1972).

Alternatives (a) and (b) are the least probable for two main reasons: firstly the Committee appointed by the States in 1827 clearly found that all existing sealed measures were considerably larger than either of these figures and they specifically refer to measures 'used in all antiquity'; secondly the examination of a large number of still existing vessels, the details of some of which are set out in Appendix 1, show figures greatly in excess in all cases. Alternatives (c) and (d) show a difference of 20 ccs or just under 2%. However, the basis of the latter capacity is entirely unknown and the Viscount, generally so comprehensive in his letters and diaries, appears to make no mention of it at all. Perhaps by chance the 1828 copper quart (which seems not now to exist) had been incorrectly made and the new 1845 brass standard was simply copied from it.

In any case, (i) in the light of the States directive of 1828, (ii) the clear evidence of the Committee of 1827 in regard to the capacities of then existing old sealed measures and (iii) the measurements which we ourselves have made on a large number of still extant specimens, alternative (c) is taken as the basic standard to be adopted for the calculations of the six sizes of Jersey flagons and measures, which should therefore have the following minimum capacities to the nearest cubic centimetre: pot 2,049 ccs, quart 1,024 ccs, pint 512 ccs, half-pint 256 ccs, noggin 128 ccs and half-noggin 64 ccs.

Purely as a broad basis of comparison, the average capacities of all specimens that we have tested in the various sizes are as follows: pot 2,140 ccs, quart 1,074 ccs, pint 530 ccs, half-pint 260 ccs, noggin 128 ccs and half-noggin 64 ccs. Naturally, averages alone can be 'suspect' and, for those interested, Appendix I provides some indication of the actual range of capacities encountered. The averages show merely that in no case is a 'size' below its basic standard; that the smaller sizes are very close to the standard, and that the percentage over-burden increases in the larger sizes, which for safety in manufacture might well be expected, particularly at a time when great accuracy of capacity would have been no part of a pewterer's normal manufacturing process. Even today, with relatively precise machine manufacture, a small percentage excess is allowed on beer measures according to size.

There have been one or two individual examples measured in the smaller sizes which have been found to be marginally below the standards we have set. For this there are two very adequate explanations; firstly, the accuracy of our own measurements – no great attempt has been made to attain laboratory standards – and, secondly, distortion of the vessel, particularly denting, which is quite common. Either or both of these factors would provide an entirely adequate explanation, especially in relation to such small sizes where, as will be observed, variations of only a cubic centimetre or so are involved; variations of this order cannot be regarded as significant. It will also be noted that a very occasional piece has a capacity appreciably higher than the norm; for such pieces we have, so far, no verifiable explanation. It may be that they have no special significance, but, in any case, we certainly do not accept that they belong to an entirely separate set of standards, Imperial or otherwise, though it is just possible that some were 'adapted', or made, to conform to the higher Guernsey standard: indeed, one or two examples have been found bearing Guernsey verification seals.

Having reached the foregoing conclusions as to the actual Jersey capacity standards, their practical application and relevance must be examined bearing in mind, particularly, the two distinct types of Jersey vessels, the lidded and the unlidded, fully described in earlier chapters. The former type is more suited, prima facie, for use as a jug or storage vessel and the latter for the measurement of liquids, or perhaps as a drinking vessel. It has always been stated in the past that six sizes were made in the Jersey lidded form, but only five in the unlidded, the largest size, i.e. the pot, being non-existent, and the general absence of the larger sizes in the unlidded range (see Chapter 3), provides a further indication that such vessels were not primarily intended for the storage of liquids. One unlidded vessel of pot size has, however, now been discovered, but, in view of its apparent rarity, this does not affect the general premise.

Clearly if a vessel were intended merely for use in the home, or in the church for Holy Communion, there was no great necessity for it to be made accurately to any particular standard, any more than in the case of an ordinary, modern, household jug, nor need it have been officially checked and sealed. Where, however, vessels were to be used for the sale or measurement of specific quantities of wine, beer, cider, etc., then they were required to be submitted to the Viscount for checking against the standard, and for stamping, and would, therefore, have had to be made to conform to the appropriate capacity standard.

In theory, therefore, it should be possible to separate measures and (public) drinking mugs from 'private' flagons merely by the presence or otherwise of a verification seal. Unfortunately, however, this is no infallible guide since the operation of the control was irregular in the extreme. This is quite clear from the diary and letters of Col. Le Couteur, Viscount for over 30 years during Victoria's reign, and from the report made by one of his successors, R.R.Lempriere, to the Standards Commission in 1914. The law itself was defective, there were no funds available for operating it satisfactorily and, therefore, no staff to carry out the necessary examination and stamping, leaving aside the accuracy or otherwise of the standards themselves.

Nevertheless a check on the verification seals found on the many specimens examined does provide some interesting results, quite apart from the question of the attribution of the different types of marks to particular dates or reigns – a subject which will be discussed later in the chapter. Of all lidded vessels examined only 36% had verification seals, and in the largest size, the pot, only 15%, thus reinforcing the case for considering these types primarily as flagons rather than measures. On the other hand 86% of all unlidded vessels examined were found to have seals and therefore these types may clearly be classed as measures as we have already pointed out.

Makers of Channel Islands pewterware, and the general background of their operations, are discussed elsewhere, but it is perhaps relevant to consider in this chapter whether the arrangements for ordering and marketing were such that a particular piece would have been made specifically as a flagon or as a measure and therefore, possibly, to different standards, or, indeed (in the case of the flagon), to no particular standard at all. However, bearing in mind the very great cost and relative scarcity of moulds, that they were actually rented or used by different pewterers, and that parts of them were even made to serve for different kinds of objects, it seems certain that all vessels of a certain 'size' made by a pewterer were made from his particular – and probably only – mould, irrespective of whether the piece was to be used as a flagon or as a measure, even if this were known at the time of manufacture. It is quite inconceivable that separate sets of moulds were kept for each individual purpose and this is confirmed by the close correlation of our capacity measurements between numerous sealed and unsealed vessels. Obviously, therefore, the pewterer would ensure that his moulds for each size would produce a vessel certain to be of a capacity greater than the Island's standard so as to cater for all eventualities of use and would be most likely to err on the high side, particularly perhaps in the larger capacities. Our measurements (see Appendix I) suggest that this is just what happened.

The traditional local Jersey standards of capacity were in use in the Island from the 17th century or earlier and continued throughout the 18th and 19th centuries and well into the 20th. It has frequently been stated that Jersey measures were made to Imperial as well as to the local standard, the view apparently being held that Jersey adopted Imperial at the same time as the United Kingdom, or perhaps soon after, whilst, presumably, continuing to operate the old standard as well. This is quite incorrect! The Islands have always been extremely resistant to changes of old established customs, rights and privileges and, in fact, Imperial measure did not legally come into use in Jersey until January 1st 1919. Until that time the local Cabot standard of 1828 was still in force; of this there is ample evidence.

There are several documents of the late 19th century which make it clear that this local standard was still universally used. There were, in fact, several attempts to introduce the metric system, but without avail. A draft Bill with this object still exists, intended to be presented privately by a Deputy to the States during the last years of the century: this reiterates that the existing Jersey measures conformed neither to Imperial nor metric Standard. As late as 1914 the then Viscount was making strong representations to the Standards Commission in the United Kingdom about local Jersey measures and, in his reports, he refers repeatedly to '*my*' standard half-noggin, etc., these being the standards that he was still using for checking–standards which still exist and which conform to the local Cabot-based capacity system.

Nevertheless English tavern type measures made to Imperial standard were in use in the Island and were officially sealed (see page 62). It is, no doubt, this fact, coupled perhaps with the very occasional measure of Jersey shape of rather greater than normal capacity (though we have not yet found even one that has attained Imperial in any size), that has given the impression in certain quarters that the Imperial Standard was used in the Island. We know that the checking and sealing of measures was very haphazard and seemingly, providing the vessel attained the minimum Jersey standard (and Imperial would be up to 10% higher), it was stamped without question. We have indeed even found a very few French pichets and measures bearing Jersey verification seals: none, however, had capacities *below* the Jersey standards that we have accepted.

Jersey Verification Seals   In 1617 it was made illegal for anyone in Jersey to keep any measure which had not been checked and sealed by the Viscount: no doubt there were earlier enactments of a similar character, but this is as early as we need go for the purposes of this study. Similar laws, orders or regulations were reiterated at intervals during the next 300 years, and so it is fair to say that there has always been officially in force a requirement of this kind. The Viscount was (and is) an officer appointed by the English Crown and not by the States of Jersey, a situation which applies otherwise only to the Bailiff of the Island and the two Law Officers, the Attorney General and the Solicitor General. He was directly responsible for weights and measures from the earliest times right up until almost the end of the second decade of the present century, at which time a Department of Weights and Measures was set up under the local administration: even thereafter he was still the titular officer until 1967.

With these regulations for checking and sealing in force from at least the early 17th century, one might hope to find pewter or other vessels with marks that could be attributed to one or other of the Stuart monarchs – especially in the light of the close connection that some of them had with the Island – or at least to William III or Anne in whose reigns certain of the now long-established English standards for ale and wine were set. In fact the only seals found on any vessels, pewter or otherwise, are those containing the initials G R or E R, the latter referring to Edward VII. *

There are four main 'G R' seals, each quite different from the others, which we have endeavoured to date and elucidate. However, there also appear to be die varieties within some of the main marks, exhibiting small differences in the letters or surmounting crown. It is not clear whether these are actual variations made as a result of a legal change of the mark, or to a new set of punches being made (or more than one set being in use at the same time), or, again, whether they are, in some cases, merely apparent differences due to careless striking, the uneven surface of the vessel, or the nature of the metal. The close, almost microscopic examination and measurement of every example which would be necessary to make a worthwhile study is quite outside the scope of this work. In any case we have no reason at present to believe that such a study would materially add to our general knowledge of the history or dating of Channel Islands pewter.

The Seal, of which two varieties are shown in Fig. 21 and Plate XXIII, and which for identification purposes we shall designate Seal 'A', we believe to be the earliest so far discovered. As to its terminal date, we know for certain that an entirely different seal was established in 1754 and used immediately, or very soon, thereafter. For its earliest date of application it is possible to speculate from the evidence of certain flagon Groups. Thus it has not been found on any piece which can categorically be identified as belonging to Group 1, a Group for which we have suggested a terminal date of 1725 or perhaps a little later. However, there are a small number of pieces stamped with this Seal which just possibly might belong to this Group, but about which there is some doubt, either because they possess only a few of the essential Group characteristics, because parts are missing, damaged, or have been repaired so that their original characteristics have been obscured, or because they are of one of the smaller sizes, where, as has been pointed out (page 31), Group subdivisions may become blurred. Even if any of these pieces are of Group 1, they could well have been sealed some time after manufacture. On the other hand, *ALL* flagons of Group 2, with the touch IN inside the lid, which we have examined, have been found to be stamped with Seal 'A' and this Group we have dated from 1725 onwards. If our dating is correct, therefore, it would seem that this Seal probably came into use just about the end of the Group 1 period and the beginning of Group 2 and, thus, the accession to the throne of

*New seals were introduced when Elizabeth II came to the throne and again in 1967, but these are not germane to our enquiry. For the sake of completeness, however, they are listed later.

Seal 'A'

Fig. 21 Jersey verification Seal 'A'. *c.* 1727–1754. (2 varieties)

XXIII

a. Jersey verification seal 'A' (two varieties).

b. Jersey verification seals 'B', 'D' and 'E'.

c. Jersey verification seal 'C'.

d. Jersey verification seals 'E' and of Elizabeth II

74

George II, in 1727, could provide a feasible explanation.

This Seal is one of those mentioned above where die varieties seem to exist: in particular the crown appears to vary between a very crude representation and a better formed, though still primitive type. This could be explained, if indeed the seal was used for some 27 years from 1727 to 1754, by the need for periodic replacement or re-engraving of the punch, with the workmanship gradually becoming more skilled.

As already mentioned, all Group 2 flagons, with the mark IN, which we have examined have been stamped with this Seal, and in every case it has been struck on the edge of the lip on the LEFT hand side of the vessel, looking from the handle towards the front. It has also been found on about 20% of Group 3 flagons (those of John de St. Croix), but in this Group struck sometimes on the left side of the lip and sometimes on the right. Whether any significance can be attached to the position of the Seal has not yet been determined, but it could be, in the light of the Group 2 custom, that those Group 3 vessels sealed on the left side are the earlier, though we have no evidence of this. In any case all vessels with this Seal must have been made before 1754 when it was officially superseded – or just possibly by the following year if there was a short time-lag before the new seal was actually made and brought into use. The latest dated flagon that we have found with this Seal is a 'pot' by de St. Croix, inscribed ILR⚭SGF 1751 – almost certainly a 'marriage' piece.

Seal 'A', except in one special instance (see footnote),* never seems to be found in combination with any other seal on the same vessel, so that it would appear that, once stamped therewith, the flagon was always afterwards accepted as being of the legal standard; this, as we shall see, is not so in the case of other seals which very frequently are found in combination. One single piece has been found with Seal 'A' stamped twice, side by side, but one stamping is poor and this may merely be a case of a 'second shot'.

This Seal is shown in Fig. 22 and Plate XXIII. It came into use officially in 1754. We have, earlier in this Chapter, referred to the Regulations regarding capacities promulgated in that year. They were part of a comprehensive code governing all kinds of weights and measures and establishing a whole series of new marks to be used by the Viscount. The original document showing these marks, explaining their uses and setting out fines to be levied for their evasion, still exists and has been examined. The capacity mark for the Cabot and its derivatives is that shown here as Seal 'B'. It will be noted that the crown is of standard graphical form and is much more realistic than that of Seal 'A', and that the letters G R are smaller and more even.

*One flagon has been found with Seal 'A' on the left and Seal 'B' on the right. However, the owner, now nearing 80 years of age, states that the latter Seal was stamped when he was a small boy (presumably c. 1900) when they were selling cider from the family farm. He also owns another Jersey lidded piece and a Normandy pichet, both bearing Seal 'B', which are said to have been stamped at the same time.

Seal 'B'

Fig. 22 Jersey verification Seal 'B'. 1754–1901.

We know that this Seal was used in the last few years of the reign of George II and also during the whole of that of George III. Furthermore we have every reason to believe that it was used also throughout the reigns of George IV (with a possible reservation in regard to Seal 'C'), William IV and Victoria as

(i) it is frequently found on English types of Imperial measures (i.e. post 1826) which were in use in Jersey (see Chapter 3) and also on a few pre-Imperial,

(ii) it is found on Victorian copper measures,

(iii) one of our older inhabitants states that he remembers it being struck on his family's pewter around the end of Victorian times and

(iv) we have yet to find a W R or a V R seal on Jersey pewter.

This Seal, 'B', has been found on less than 10% of all lidded (or originally lidded) vessels examined, that is on only about a quarter of those *actually sealed*, the remaining three quarters of the sealed pieces having Seal 'A' (except for three isolated specimens with Seal 'C', referred to later). This could very well suggest that the majority of Jersey lidded vessels were made before 1754, especially as it is very likely that checking and sealing would have been more strictly enforced after the new Regulations had come into force than before. Furthermore, even vessels with this Seal could very well have been made much earlier, the Seal being applied only when the vessel came into use as a measure: we have already noted some evidence of this happening (see footnote, page 75). Another fact that may tend to reinforce this idea is that more than a third of those originally lidded vessels that are stamped with this Seal have now lost their lids. It seems reasonable to assume that an unlidded vessel would have been of greater advantage than a lidded when it was generally in use for measuring liquids and it is, therefore, at least a possibility either that the lids were removed when the pieces became used as measures or, alternatively, that they were made into measures simply because the lids had been lost. It is conceiveable, too, that, if an *unlidded* piece were found to be of too large a capacity, the rim could be shortened somewhat.

It is perhaps worthy of comment that out of the very considerable number of Group 3 flagons examined – a Group which we have suggested probably extended until 1765 – only one identifiable piece had this Seal. However, some of those with lids now missing may have been made by de St. Croix, and therefore belong to this Group, and the same may be true in the case of some of the smaller sizes without a touchmark (see Page 31). Nevertheless, with 20% of the flagons in this Group having Seal 'A' and the remaining 80% having none at all (with but one certain exception) there is at least a presumption that the majority of de St. Croix's flagons, certainly in the larger sizes, were made before 1754.*

*An alternative explanation (for which, however, we have no supporting evidence of any kind) could be that for some considerable time after 1754 only *unlidded* vessels were generally accepted as measures and that lidded flagons continued to be made primarily for domestic purposes. Such a theory could place some of the extant unlidded pieces earlier than we have suggested.

Although Seal 'B' has been found on so few lidded flagons, it is generally found on unlidded measures: indeed, it is quite rare to find a sealed, unlidded piece that does not have this stamp. It is very frequently accompanied by Seals 'D' and 'E' (both of which relate to the 20th century) and is also sometimes duplicated. If struck once only, it is invariably found on the right side of the lip (looking from the handle forward), but the second striking appears on the left hand side. It has also been found struck on the blind hinge boss of a Type (a) measure. This duplication and combination with other Seals, generally not found in the case of Seal 'A', suggests a tightening of the regulations with periodical rechecking. When found in combination with Seals 'D' and 'E' it is always the nearest to the handle and, even when struck alone, it is usually very close to the junction of the top of the handle with the body. It is sometimes the only Jersey seal found on English Imperial measures: this might suggest that these measures were not always acceptable for rechecking after 1901 and whilst the local standard was still in force. This Seal has also been found on a Guernsey Type I pint (see Plate XXIV), a Guernsey Type II quart, several Normandy pichets and measures of typical shouldered form and a small French flagon of a type found in the St. Malo region.

As in the case of Seal 'A' there are apparent die varieties in Seal 'B', particularly in the crown itself. Some of these variations may, in fact, be unreal and due merely to how the seal was struck or to the shape, metal or surface texture of the vessel not allowing a perfect strike, but other examples seem quite definitely to have been struck with a different die, and this would indeed be expected if this particular type of Seal was used, as we believe, for nearly 150 years.

Seal 'C'

This Seal, shown in Fig. 23 and Plate XXIII is something of a mystery. It has so far been found on only five vessels, two Group 3 pots, a Group 4 quart, a Type (a), blind hinge boss, unlidded quart, and a St. Malo pichet, probably of the early 19th century. Its presence on the last three, and its general sophistication and form, suggest that it is unlikely to be older than the second half of the reign of George III and it could even be that it relates to that of George IV, though we have no supporting evidence. Alternatively, it may be that it was a type of stamp more generally used at some time on a different form of measure. We know that the Viscount had different sized stamps for different purposes just as the Department of Weights and Measures has today. As will be seen, it is considerably larger and bolder than either Seal 'A' or Seal 'B' (Figs. 21, 22 and 23 being drawn to the same scale). On all five examples it was struck on the right hand side of the vessel and was not accompanied by any other seal.

Fig. 23 Jersey verification Seal 'C'. ? c. 1790–1830.

Seal 'D'

Fig. 24 Jersey verification Seal 'D'. 1902–1910.

Fig. 25 Jersey verification Seal 'E'. 1910–1952.

Seal 'E'

This Seal, shown in Fig. 24 and Plate XXIII, presents no difficulty. It relates to the reign of Edward VII, 1902 to 1910. It has not been found on any lidded vessel,* but is seen on a high percentage of unlidded measures, frequently in conjunction with Seals 'B' and 'E', or with 'E' only. In the former case it is struck *between* the other two and in the latter it is nearer the handle than the other seal. As in the case of Seal 'B' it is sometimes found duplicated, the second striking being on the left hand side of the lip. Where struck only once it has always been found on the right hand side. No die varieties have been noted in this Seal.

This Seal, shown in Fig. 25 and Plate XXIII, relates not only to the reign of George V, 1910 to 1936, but also to that of George VI, 1936 to 1952 and, thus, was used both before and after the Imperial standard was adopted in the Island. As previously stated, it is found in association with Seals 'B' and 'D', being always the one farthest away from the

XXIV Guernsey pint flagon with Jersey verification seal 'B'. Note that the neck of this piece has been cut down to conform to the lower Jersey capacity.

*but Gill Wylie in *Pewter, Measure for Measure* speaks of a Guernsey pot with 'the excise marks of Edward and George II'.

handle, on the right hand side of the lip. It is also found duplicated, being then struck on the left hand side. It has not been found on any lidded measures, and no die varieties have been noted.

Although the foregoing completes the list of seals found on Jersey pewter, we feel that to bring the reader up to date, we should mention two further seals which have come into use subsequently. Both are shown in Plate xxiii: the first, with the letters E II R surmounted by a crown and with J beneath, came into use in 1953 at the beginning of the present Queen's reign and, the second, an adaptation of the Jersey coat of arms, came into force in 1967 when the Viscount ceased to be the titular head of the Weights and Measures Department, which was then transferred to the administration of the Public Works Committee of the States of Jersey. Collectors will be interested to compare this Seal with John de St. Croix's touch as recorded on the London touchplate.

Strictly, as far as Guernsey is concerned, we need hardly be concerned with the Island's legal capacity system and its history since all pewter measures were specifically forbidden from 1611 onwards. That this law was adhered to for a very long time is confirmed by the fact that, with the exception of one Sark Seigneurial piece, none of the standard skirted Guernsey Type I flagons, which appear to comprise more than three quarters of the total of Guernsey lidded vessels, have any verification seals – a clear indication that, in fact, they were not used as measures.

However, some Type II flagons do bear Guernsey seals as also do a few unlidded Jersey measures, one or two rare Jersey lidded flagons and one or two possible 'hybrids'. It is therefore desirable that we should give some account of the sizes and standards involved and of the verification seals used.

As early as 1581 there was concern about the accuracy of weights and measures in Guernsey, and in the following year it was decreed that any pot, quart, pint and half-pint used for the retailing of beverages or liquor should be marked with the stamps of the rose and the fleur-de-lys 'which the Procureur (States Official) carries for that purpose'.

In 1611 a complete code of laws for weights and measures was laid down and this does not seem to have altered significantly during at least the next two hundred years. As regards capacity, the law, in addition to setting out certain standards and reiterating the essential requirements of checking and sealing, states that 'all measures of pewter are forbidden on penalty (of a fine) of 60 sous tournois'. In 1614 all existing gauges and standards for measures were ordered to be called in to ensure uniformity in the future: no doubt any pewter measures then existing would have been destroyed. On numerous occasions subsequently, the requirements for checking and sealing were repeated – in 1617–18 (when the sizes of

Guernsey Capacities and Seals

pot, quart, pint and half-pint were again mentioned), in 1623, 1627, 1637–38 and 1668. Later, in 1717, it was specifically decreed that only Guernsey Island sizes could be used, and in 1719–20 there was a further repetition of the sealing requirement with reference to the sizes of pot, quart, pint, half-pint, quarto* and demi-quarto,* the last two being sizes which we have not encountered in relation to proven Guernsey pewter. These rules and regulations in regard to capacity seem generally to have remained unchanged throughout the 18th century and indeed during the whole of the 19th century and part of the 20th century as well, for, as in the case of Jersey, the local capacity system continued in force until ultimately superseded by the Imperial Standard, in this Island early in 1917, nearly two years ahead of Jersey.

There is one point of special interest concerning Guernsey and it is that the actual Standards, both for capacity and other measures, belonged to the British Crown. From the time of James I they were rented by the Crown to the Royal Court of Guernsey who, in turn, sublet them to their Inspector. This practice continued until 1830 when they were again rented by the Crown; this time, however, not to the Royal Court but to the States (Parliament) of the Island, who, in 1832, rented them to their own Inspector, John Cochrane, members of whose family continued to carry out these duties until 1917. Many of the original Standards of the early 17th century still exist and can be seen in the Lukis Museum in Guernsey.

In the foregoing historical notes certain sizes have been mentioned several times, namely the pot, quart, pint and half-pint – not, of course, referring to pewter vessels but usually, no doubt, to copper or brass. Nevertheless, as would be clearly logical, pewter flagons were generally made to similar sizes. In the past it has always been firmly stated that Guernsey lidded pewter flagons exist in only the three sizes of pot, quart and pint. However, as we have already pointed out in Chapter 2, rare examples of the Type II flagon have been found in the half-pint size also. Moreover, only very recently, a few rare half-pints have been found, some marked by Joseph Wingod, a well-known maker of Type I flagons, and having most of the Type I characteristics, but without the typical skirt (see Chapter 5) and others, of entirely typical form, with the marks of AD and 'Carter'. It should, therefore, be accepted that both Types of Guernsey flagons exist in *at least* four sizes, viz: pot, quart, pint and half-pint, with the last rare or very rare.

As to the actual standard capacities of these sizes, we are fortunate to have a ready and reliable reference in the work entitled *The Channel Islands* by Professor David Anstead F.R.S. and Dr. Robert Latham, F.R.S., written about 1860. The authors state that they took great care to ensure that all their information was accurate, and, to this end, that

*presumably the equivalent of the Jersey noggin and half-noggin.

Professor Anstead spent four years in Guernsey. Both were men of high repute and could well have had access to information and material no longer available. A completely new study of Island capacities from primary sources would therefore be quite unjustified, especially in view of its limited relevance to Guernsey pewter.

These authors quote as the basic Island capacity standard the Guernsey Wine Gallon, which, they state, contained 264 cubic inches Imperial or, in certain circumstances for excise purposes 261 cubic inches. The former basis gives a gallon of 4326 cubic centimetres and therefore a pot of 2163 ccs, a quart of 1081 ccs, a pint of 540 ccs and a half-pint of 270 ccs. The latter basis gives figures of 4255 ccs, 2127 ccs, 1064 ccs, 532 ccs and 266 ccs respectively, to the nearest cc. The Guernsey flagons that we have examined and measured have capacities varying between 2116 ccs and 2175 ccs in the pot size, 1070 ccs and 1125 ccs in the quart, and 523 ccs and 608 ccs in the pint size, though only three rather unusual pieces (see Chapter 5) have the latter very high capacity. The few rare half-pint pieces vary between 270 ccs and 275 ccs. In each case these empirical results show a reasonable relationship to the standards quoted by Anstead and Latham, especially bearing in mind that these vessels were not generally made as measures. The lower of the two standards (i.e. based on the 261 cubic inch gallon) seems the more applicable since it conforms more closely to the minimum capacities. Considering only those Guernsey lidded flagons in the three larger sizes actually sealed* with the official verification marks (all Type II pieces with the exception of 'the Sark flagon'), the range of capacity found, size for size, is much narrower, viz from 2150 ccs to 2175 ccs in the pot, 1075 ccs to 1090 ccs in the quart and 550 ccs to 555 ccs in the pint, again suggesting that the lower value of the wine standard was used, since some of the sealed and accepted pieces would fail to 'pass' the higher standard. In relation to Guernsey pewter, therefore, we have adopted the following well-established capacity standards:

> pot 2127 ccs, quart 1064 ccs, pint 532 ccs and half-pint 266 ccs, in each case to the nearest cc.

We have also referred to certain Jersey type unlidded measures and a very few Jersey lidded pieces, which have been found bearing Guernsey verification seals: these were all in the small sizes of noggin and half-noggin (see Plate XXVI) and in every case the capacity 'passed' the standard adopted above.

Guernsey verification seals present a far simpler problem than those of Jersey. As we have seen, in 1581 it was laid down that all measures must be stamped with the rose and the fleur-de-lys and these are, in fact, the only seals that we have ever found on any Guernsey pewter,* which,

*It must be accepted that, in this instance, the empirical information is somewhat restricted owing to the relatively small number of Guernsey flagons on which verification seals have been found.

*Two Guernsey flagons have been found with Jersey seals, presumably having been brought into that Island at some time and accepted there. Both are still in Jersey.

Guernsey Verification Seals

xxv

a. Guernsey verification seal of 'rose'.

b. Guernsey verification seal of 'fleur-de-lys'.

c. Modern Guernsey verification seals.

for this purpose, includes the unlidded Jersey Type (b) measures and the rare Jersey lidded pieces with these seals. It should be made clear that the sealing operation included *both* devices, i.e. they were not alternatives. One device was stamped on the left side of the lip and the other on the right, but the same device is not consistently on the same side. Very occasionally both stamps are duplicated, presumably a subsequent verification. The seals are shown in Plate xxv.

Whilst this of itself is quite straightforward, what we do not know is when pewter vessels became permissible as measures in Guernsey, and when, consequently, their stamping with the local verification seals began. One possible theory is that this took place following the States taking over the renting of the Royal Standards in 1830 and appointing their own Inspector in 1832, an arrangement of special interest to which we have already drawn attention earlier in this Chapter. We have so far been unable to secure any positive evidence to support this theory but, taking all the known facts into account, the explanation seems plausible pending any more acceptable alternative.

To bring the subject of verification seals in Guernsey up to date we illustrate also in Plate xxv an example of the GU system which came into force with the Imperial Standard in 1917 and is still in use. This seal includes the last two figures of the year and a letter for the month.

To conclude this Chapter, we append a table showing (in cubic centimetres) the capacity standards we have adopted for Jersey and Guernsey in comparison with three English Standards, viz: Old English Wine, Old English Ale and Imperial. It will be noted that of these five

c

standards, Imperial has the highest capacity, being, 'size' for 'size', about 2% larger than the Old English Ale and about $6\frac{1}{2}$% larger than the Guernsey: the latter is nearly 4% larger than the Jersey, which, itself, is some $12\frac{1}{2}$% greater than the Old English Wine. It would seem, therefore, that all three English standards are sufficiently removed from those of the two Channel Islands to avoid any real difficulty in deciding whether a flagon or measure was made with the intention of conforming to a Channel Islands, or to an English standard.

The table also shows the names given to the various Channel Islands sizes, and those generally used for the 'equivalent' English range.

XXVI Unusual Jersey half-noggin with Guernsey verification seal and of 'Guernsey' capacity.

CHANNEL ISLANDS CAPACITY STANDARDS & NOMENCLATURE			ENGLISH CAPACITY STANDARDS & NOMENCLATURE			
Size	Jersey	Guernsey	Old English Wine	Old English Ale	Imperial	Size
Pot	2048	2127	1893	2224	2272	*Half-Gallon*
Quart	1024	1064	947	1112	1136	*Quart*
Pint	512	534	473	556	568	*Pint*
Half Pint	256	266	237	278	284	*Half-Pint*
Noggin	128	(133)*	118	139	142	*Gill*
Half Noggin	64	$(66\frac{1}{2})$*	59	$69\frac{1}{2}$	71	*Half Gill*

NOTE—Capacities are in cubic centimetres, generally to the nearest cc.

*No certain examples of these sizes have been found in Guernsey pewter. One old Guernsey regulation applies the names 'quarto' and 'demi-quarto' to these sizes and not 'noggin' and 'half-noggin'.

83

5

A Mixed Bag

Having now completed the general survey of Channel Island measures and flagons, we shall, in this chapter, be discussing a few individual pieces of special interest. We shall also examine other items of pewterware made by Channel Islands pewterers, in the widest interpretation of that term, and used in the Islands. In this respect we are limited to plates and a very few porringers, these being the only items about which we can be certain – by reason of identifiable touches.

In Chapter 1, reference was made to one or two rare flagons, generally of English baluster form but having certain Channel Islands' characteristics: the first piece to be examined is one of these examples. It is illustrated in Plate xxvii and is 152 millimetres (6″) high to the lip with a capacity of 568 cubic centimetres. As will be seen it has a twin acorn thumbpiece, generally unknown in English pewter, but typical of the Channel Islands and of many French patterns. The wedge or tongue, too, is reminiscent of the Channel Islands style (particularly that of Guernsey), and so is the handle, but the lid is circular (with a small 'point' at the front) instead of the so-called heart-shape universally found in the Channel Islands. The general shape of the body is closer to the Jersey than the Guernsey form, but it has a much less pronounced neck and a less rounded belly than either: the capacity is higher than any Jersey piece that we have ever found, but some Guernsey pieces are even higher. The initials, stamped on top of the lid after the Guernsey custom, are of typical Channel Island syllabic form – I D G – which could stand for Jean de Garis. This piece was in the collection of the late, Mr. R.F. Michaelis. A second apparently similar piece has been seen in a photograph of part of a collection believed to have belonged to Mr. H.M. Cooke, of London, but its whereabouts are not now known.

There is, however, in the author's collection, another piece (see Plate xxviii) which, as will be seen by comparison with Plate xxvii, is of almost identical shape to the preceding piece, with the same pattern of decorative lines and a similar handle. The lid is actually slightly more pointed at the front (i.e. nearer a Channel Islands shape) and has stamped on it the initials MGR (perhaps Marie Gerard in the Channel Islands initialling system). The wedge is similar to that on Mr. Michaelis' flagon but the thumbpiece is quite different – very interestingly so – being of a twin-bud pattern (see Plate XXVIII) very similar in shape to that found on some Guernsey quarts, though here slightly decorated. Interestingly too, this piece is also a quart, 200 mm in height and with a capacity of 1080 ccs – in the Channel Islands range rather than the English, as may be seen from an examination of the comparative table at the end of Chapter 4. The vessel is jointed vertically (as is the preceding piece) and not horizontally as otherwise found on Channel Islands flagons.* In Appendix V we have examined both this piece and the preceding one in considerable detail, especially in relation to their relevance to Channel Islands pewter. We have come to the conclusion that they must be regarded as Guernsey pieces – probably the earliest yet found – and dated between 1690 and 1720.

Next we have selected for special mention a group of five Jersey flagons, four of which certainly, and the other possibly, have close affinities. The first is the piece that we have previously called 'the St. John's flagon', illustrated in Plate XXIX. It is a pot having virtually all the special characteristics typical of Group 1. Its essential details are set out in Appendix II together with those of the following four pieces. It is of great interest and importance because of its dated inscription, reading: 'DONNE A L'EGLISE DE ST. IEAN 1718', (see Plate XXX), and because it bears the touch P:D:R, which we ascribe to Pierre du Rousseau. Associated with this piece is a second flagon of pot size, also in the possession of St. John's Parish Church in Jersey with, stamped on the lid, the inscription 'POUR LA PARROISSE DE ST IAN'. This flagon is virtually identical in all other respects to the dated flagon, including capacity, and, although it does not bear any touch on the lid, there can be no doubt that it is a companion piece for Holy Communion by the same maker. The third related piece is a quart in the writer's ownership, with the same touch of P:D:R on the lid: it has most of the characteristics of the two pots and is clearly also by the same maker (see Plate XXXI). The fourth piece in this group is another pot (see Plate XXXII, on the lid of which are stamped the initials P:D in an incuse rectangle, one end of which clearly has chamfered corners, but the other is so imperfectly struck as to be unrecognisable. Macrophotography has, however, convinced us beyond reasonable doubt that this is an incomplete P:D:R mark, the form of the letters and the positions of the 'dot' and 'colon' being seemingly identical to those in du Rousseau's touch. This view is maintained even though the touch is struck in a quite different position on the lid from that on the other examples and some of the characteristics of the vessel are dissimilar; in particular it has a pronounced projecting fillet around

*English vessels, also, almost invariably have horizontal seaming, but *early* French and other Continental pieces are found with vertical joints.

XXVII A rare baluster measure of pint capacity with twin-acorn thumbpiece, possibly attributable to the Channel Islands (see Page 84 and Appendix v). Compare with more typical English baluster in Plate II.

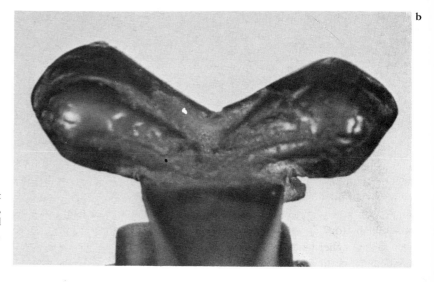

XXVIII

a. A rare baluster measure of quart capacity with twin-bud thumbpiece, possibly attributable to the Channel Islands (see Page 84 and Appendix v). Compare with Plates II and XXVII.

b. Detail of twin-bud thumbpiece.

xxx Lid of flagon shown in Plate xxix

xxix The earliest dated Jersey lidded (Communion) flagon (Group 1) from St. John's Parish Church, Jersey, 1718; maker PDR.

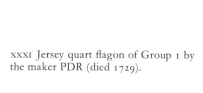

xxxi Jersey quart flagon of Group 1 by the maker PDR (died 1729).

xxxii Pot sized Jersey flagon with touchmark PD(?) on lid: this is probably an incomplete striking of the touchmark PDR. Note fillet round neck joint.

the neck, but no incised lines at the lip or elsewhere.

The final piece in this group is another pot flagon, also with the touch-mark P:D:R struck on the lid in the same position as on the St. John's piece. Particular points of interest about this piece are, (i) its height – it is some 20 mm taller than either of the other pots with this mark, although it has approximately the same capacity due, no doubt, to the fairly deep 'well' under the flagon, (ii) whilst it has incised lines at the lip, belly and base, it has a single, reeded, slightly raised band around the neck, and (iii) it has the initials MHR die-stamped on the lid, each in its own incuse square, a type of initialling which we have not seen on any other Channel Islands piece.

For purely local reasons, mention must now be made of three entirely typical Group 3 Jersey flagons, two pots and a pint, all made by John de St. Croix, and having, stamped on their handles, the inscription 'ST LORAIN' (St. Lawrence). Clearly they were originally used as Communion flagons, probably having been bought, or presented, for that purpose about the time of their manufacture, and they are still in the possession of St. Lawrence Parish Church in Jersey. Plate XXXIII shows these three pieces together with a plate and two alms dishes, also by de St. Croix and also belonging to the same church – the only church in Jersey with examples of his work. It is known that a large branch of the de St. Croix family lived in this Parish (most of the rest being in the main town of St. Helier), and it is at least possible that these pieces were actually presented by the family – perhaps even by the pewterer himself, though unfortunately we have not found a 'Jean de Ste. Croix' in the Parish records of the appropriate time and age.

Turning now to unlidded measures, none seem worthy of special mention, though note should be taken of the two examples of an unusual $1\frac{1}{2}$ pints (Jersey) size with capacities of 780 and 781 ccs respectively (see Chapter 3). It may also be of interest to record, because of their inscriptions, a set of three pieces of Type (b), comprising a pint, a half-pint and a noggin, with '*P. Pafsons*' engraved around the belly in the type of italic script usually found on English tavernware; this name has not, so far, been traced in the Islands. The fact remains, however, that these three pieces are all stamped with Jersey verification seals 'B' and 'D', indicating their use in the Island in the 19th century, or even a little earlier, and also during the first years of this century. Their capacities are 528 ccs, 260 ccs, and 129 ccs respectively, very close indeed to the official Jersey standards (see Chapter 4).

Generally unlidded Channel Islands pieces do not bear inscriptions, except, very occasionally, owner's initials stamped, engraved or crudely scratched somewhere on the body or handle. We have, however, seen two English lidless tavern mugs of the Old English Wine Standard,

XXXIV Early Guernsey pint flagon by unknown maker, touchmark AD.—no strut to handle.

XXXIII A group of pewter by John de St. Croix in St. Lawrence Parish Church, Jersey.

*Gill Wylie, *Pewter, Measure for Measure.*

probably of the first quarter of the 19th century, which, although not stamped with any Jersey seal, and certainly not conforming to the local standard, appear to have been used by some enterprising local publican as they bear, on the front in the usual italic script, the inscription 'W. Margan, Perseverance Inn, Jersey', contained within an oval border. We should also record a pair of English Imperial pints of the late 19th century with Seals 'B', 'D' and 'E' and inscribed 'NAVY HOTEL, ST. HELIER, JERSEY'.

Turning now to Guernsey, we have already mentioned 'the Sark flagon' by Thomas (?) Ingles, whose touch appears in Plate LV. This piece does not differ very significantly from the general pattern of Type I Guernseys (see Plate I) except in having the handle affixed directly to the body at the lower end. Its statistics are set out in Appendix III. Two other similar pieces examined are apparently by the same maker and these three, together with a pint flagon bearing the same touch, are probably amongst the earliest Guernsey pieces yet found.

Possibly of similar period is the flagon illustrated in Plate XXXIV: it is one of only four pieces so far traced, three having been found and examined by the authors and the third mentioned by Wylie.* Three are pints and the other a so-far unique half-pint: all bear the touch AD within a heart (see Plate LII). This piece has been selected for special mention not only because of the apparent rarity of the touch, but also because of its location *inside* the lid, a position not so far found

xxxv Rare Guernsey half-pint flagon by
J. Wingod; c. 1725.

xxxvı Unidentified half-pint flagon from
Sark Seigneurial Collection. (By per-
mission of the Dame of Sark).
(Photo: P. Hudson, Sark).

on any other Guernsey flagons, and because it is relief-cast and not die struck as are all other touches that we have found. That this is indeed a touch and not an owner's or other mark, we have no doubt: the very fact that it is relief-cast, i.e. cast from a mould in which the mark has been cut or struck, in reverse, virtually guarantees this, quite apart from its general appearance and the fact that four examples are known. Although in other ways this flagon, and its companions, are broadly of standard Type I form, there are, on all, some detail points of particular interest, viz: (i) the handle is fixed directly to the body without a strut, (ii) the 'decoration' at both the neck and belly is achieved by two incised lines each side of what appears to be merely a raised body joint, quite different from the usual three reeded bands, (iii) there are additional, uncommon incised lines at the lip and at the bottom of the neck, (iv) the wedge on the lid somewhat resembles the Jersey form and (v) the capacity of the pints is high – at 608 ccs the highest we have ever found in a Channel Island flagon of this 'size'. We are unable to suggest any maker for these pieces or indeed to say for certain where they were made. Virtually all other Type I flagons of which we have knowledge must have been made in England, but these four are sufficiently different to admit alternative possibilities, for example local manufacture in the Island itself.

No other Guernsey Type I pot, quart or pint yet found seems worthy of individual mention, but a few half-pints (a rare size, as we have already indicated) have been discovered, two (by AD and Carter) clearly of this Type and others certainly related thereto but having certain different characteristics. The latter pieces, one of which is illustrated in Plate xxxv are 126 mm. (5″) high to the lip and have a capacity of 270 ccs, a 'standard' Guernsey capacity (see Chapter 4). The thumbpiece, wedge and lid are all of the usual Guernsey form and the latter bears on top the touch of Joseph Wingod, a well-known maker of Type I flagons in other sizes. The handle, too, is of standard shape, but the hinge is five flanged (i.e. two on the lid and three at the top of the handle) and not of the almost universal Channel Island three-flanged pattern. The decorative treatment around the neck and belly of these pieces takes the form merely of sets of four incised lines instead of the more usual raised bands. The great difference, however, between these small flagons and any Guernsey piece yet found in the three larger sizes, is that the distinctive, projecting skirt is completely absent and the base resembles much more closely the gradual everted shape of the Jersey pattern. There is, however, a deep 'well', typical of Guernsey, beneath the flagon and not the shallow 'Jersey' type. The vessels have been microscopically examined to see if the bases could previously have been of skirted form and subsequently reset, but there is no sign of this whatsoever. Although the general shape appears less curvaceous than the Guernsey and thus more akin to the Jersey, detail measurements have shown that this is, in fact, not so and that it is merely an illusion produced by the absence of a skirt and of the deep inversion of the bottom of the belly from which the skirt normally springs (see Fig. 26). Despite this essential difference in base configuration, we consider that these rare pieces must definitely be classified as Guernsey flagons, basically of Type I, and probably made early in Wingod's career, say before 1730. One piece is stamped twice with the Guernsey verification seals of rose and fleur-de-lys.

Another, and yet more unusual half-pint (see Plate XXXVI) belongs to the Seigneurie of Sark. It is 132 mm tall and has a 'Guernsey' capacity of 275 ccs; it is stamped with the Guernsey verification seals of rose and fleur-de-lys and bears on the lid the initials N L P, standing for Nicolas le Pelley, Seigneur of the Island from 1733 to 1742. Clearly, therefore, it was made within this period or earlier and the presence of the Guernsey verification seals, as in the case of the 'Ingles' flagon, demonstrates the especial position of Sark in relation to Guernsey, where these seals were certainly not used on pewter at that time. This piece has engraved lines around the neck, but no decoration around the belly and the foot has a rather more pronounced eversion than the Wingod pieces. There are appreciable differences between this piece and the latter and thus this example may well be by a different maker; indeed it lacks so many of the usual Guernsey Type I features that it should, perhaps, be regarded as a 'hybrid', the existence of examples of which we have already suggested.

It is here appropriate to illustrate (see Plate XXXVII) one further piece of Sark Seigneurial pewter. This is a half-noggin, 75 mm in height to the lip and with a capacity of 71 ccs, well above the normal Jersey half-noggin size (of 64 ccs), but reasonably close to a Guernsey half-noggin capacity, if such a size existed in Guernsey pewter. This piece, too, has the Guernsey verification seals stamped on the lip. Its general shape and several of its other features are rather similar to those of the Wingod half-pints already described – note particularly the incised lines at the neck and belly and the shape of the foot. The wedge is of the Guernsey type and the acorns slope slightly forward. As in the case of the preceding piece the initials of Nicolas le Pelley appear on the lid, placing it, at the latest, between 1733 and 1742. If this is accepted as a Type I Guernsey half-noggin, then there would appear to be no reason why ultimately a similar piece of noggin capacity should not be found to complete a set of six sizes, as in the case of Jersey. However, were it not for the position and form of the incised lines, and the rather high capacity, this half-noggin might easily be accepted as a small Jersey flagon; it may, therefore, also be a hybrid, especially as Sark was originally colonised from Jersey and was under the control of a Jersey Seigneur until the early 18th century.

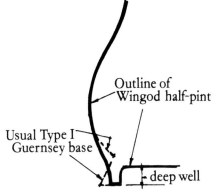

Fig. 26 Outline of rare Guernsey Type I half-pint.

Turning now to Guernsey Type II, we have noted that whilst the great majority of these flagons have been found in Guernsey itself, are of that Island's capacity, and have on the lid the initials Ns L Ct between Tudor roses with a 'GUERNESEY' label below, a few virtually identical pieces have been found in Jersey, of Jersey capacity and with no marks of any kind: we have speculated elsewhere as to their origin. Here we illustrate (see Plate XXXVIII) three specimens of the marked variety of the pot, quart and pint sizes which exhibit considerable detail differences one from another, some of which have already been briefly referred to in Chapter 2. These differences may be considered under three headings:

(a) General shape –

(i) the pot is of a particularly inferior, crude, unbalanced shape, the pint is somewhat better, though weak at the foot, but the quart has clean, well-formed lines,

(ii) the pot and pint have visibly more curved profiles than the quart,

(b) Skirt or foot –

the pot has a very rudimentary foot, much too small for the size of the flagon and crudely 'bent on' to the main body (see Fig. 27(a)). The quart, on the other hand, has a correctly sized skirt springing cleanly from the deep inversion at the bottom of the belly (see Fig. 27(b)). The pint is different from both of the others, though it more closely resembles the pot: it has a flat, outspread base with edge moulding, joined to the body by a pronounced inward curve (see Fig. 27(c)).

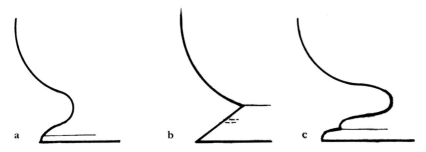

Fig. 27 Some Guernsey Type II foot shapes

a. on a pot

b. on a quart

c. on a pint.

(c) Workmanship and metal –

Although this may not be apparent from the photograph, the pot is light in weight and the metal is thin, particularly that of the lid, the impact of the stamp on top being clearly visible on the underside. Generally the 'production' of the piece seems amateurish. The quart, on the other hand, is solid and very well made, clearly by an experienced pewterer. The pint is of reasonable weight and better than the pot, but certainly not as good as the quart.

In the light of the foregoing factors it seems inconceivable that the man who made the fine quart could also have been responsible for the

XXXVII Unidentified half-noggin flagon from the Sark Seigneurial Collection. (By permission of the Dame of Sark).

XXXIX Guernsey Type II half-pint (see Page 95).

(Photo: P. Hudson, Sark).
XXXVIII Examples of pot, quart and pint sizes of Guernsey lidded flagons, Type II. Note detail differences (see Page 93).

pot and, perhaps to a lesser degree, for the pint: professional pride and skill could surely never have produced such different results. This, of course, is a conclusion that only actual physical examination of the flagons themselves can demonstrate clearly. However, somewhat similar differences have been noted in a fair proportion of Type II pieces and readers may well be able to check specimens for themselves. On this evidence alone we ourselves can only come to the conclusion that Ns L Ct (whoever he was), whose initials appear on all three lids, was not the actual maker but probably merely a dealer or agent. This view, which is supported by the unmarked pieces found in Jersey, is more fully discussed in Chapter 6.

To complete the presently known series of Type II with the GUERNESEY label, mention should be made of the rare half-pint, of which only four definite examples have so far been traced (see Plate XXXIX). Although all these pieces are quite well made and of good metal, the shape is odd and aesthetically unsatisfactory. The neck is long and out of proportion to the belly, which appears to have 'dropped', and the outline curvature seems exaggerated relative to other sizes. Details of this and other Type II pieces are included in Appendix III.

Examples of Guernsey Type II shape with no marks on the lid (or elsewhere) and with Jersey capacities have already been referred to. They have so far been found only in the sizes of pot, pint and half-pint. An example of a pint is illustrated in Plate XL on the left of a marked example of Guernsey capacity. As will be seen the outlines are virtually identical: the Jersey piece has a height of 149 mm, a wedge of 23 mm and a capacity of 518 ccs, whereas the marked 'GUERNESEY' piece is 152 mm high, has the same wedge length of 23 mm but has a capacity of 550 ccs. The Jersey piece has, scratched on the bottom, the initials CCB (probably Charles Cabot) with the date '1793' and, neatly engraved on the front, the same initials with the date '1797'.

To conclude this study of individual pieces of special interest, we now turn to a few pieces which are not completely easy to classify. They may be merely deliberate variants of either the standard Jersey or Guernsey forms due to the whim of the pewterer or his client, accidental hybrids by a maker not fully conversant with the Islands' patterns, or perhaps, very occasionally, foreign pieces which have found their way to the Islands and been used there because of their general resemblance to Channel Islands styles. Two pieces from the Sark Seigneurial pewter, a half-pint and a half-noggin, which perhaps should rightfully be included in this group, have already been mentioned, and we shall now deal briefly with four other pieces from different sources. Although by no means exhausting the list of 'hybrids' or 'rogues', they give a general idea of some of the variants encountered and it would be quite impractical to discuss here every piece exhibiting special idiosyncrasies.

The first of these four pieces is a quart (see Plate XLI), of fairly standard Jersey shape but with unusual features, viz: a series of eight inscribed lines at the lip; bands round the neck rather similar to the Guernsey style and a somewhat similar treatment, though fainter, round the belly; a wide and thick handle with virtually no strut at the foot and, finally, a very 'pointed' lid (i.e. it has an exaggerated heart shape). The wedge, however, is relatively long (41 mm) and typically Jersey, as is the slightly domed lid, and the capacity at 1095 ccs is within the Jersey range. The flagon could be of fairly late manufacture, perhaps contemporaneous with Group 4, and we regard it basically as a Jersey variant: it has no marks of any kind, no initials and no seal.

The second piece, which may be seen in the Lukis Museum in Guernsey, is a half-pint of very unusual form (see Plate XLII). It is of slim baluster shape, much less curvaceous than the normal Channel Islands form, with a skirt nearly vertical, but slightly everted at the bottom. When viewed from beneath the metal forming the skirt is rather thick and the cavity under the flagon is deep. The handle is affixed directly to the body without a strut at the lower end. The vessel has a wedge of Guernsey type, 25 mm in length, and the body has nine incised lines, one at the lip and four pairs below, which show clearly on the photograph. The lid bears owner's initials, and the lip is stamped with the Guernsey verification seals of rose and fleur-de-lys; there are no visible touch or other marks. This is certainly a problem piece and for the moment all one cay say is that, although it appears to have been accepted for use in Guernsey, its origin is very uncertain.

The next piece to be examined is shown in Plate XLIII alongside a standard Jersey piece of similar size: it is a half-noggin and conforms to the Jersey capacity standard. However, the rather 'shouldered' body shape and slight collar around the lip are rather more reminiscent of a French than a Channel Islands pattern. The handle, too, has a slightly extended terminal (not generally found on Channel Islands pewter). Absolute identification is difficult, especially in the absence of the thumb-piece, but we are inclined to assign this piece to Jersey and possibly of quite early date, perhaps even as early as the middle of the 17th Century. It may, alternatively, be more appropriately rated as a hybrid.

The final piece illustrated (see Plate XLIV), is clearly an English/Channel Islands hybrid. It is a half-pint, the body of which with its skirt, handle and stand-off strut are all Guernsey Type II, but the lid is completely circular with the English double-volute thumbpiece and fleur-de-lys tongue; it carries no marks of any kind. The hinge and hinge-pin were most carefully examined to see if any manipulation had been effected, but the whole assembly certainly seemed original.

XL Comparison photograph of Jersey *left* and Guernsey *right* Type II lidded flagons, pint size.

XLI Jersey quart flagon of unusual type: note decoration of incised lines.

XLII Unidentified small lidded flagon in the Lukis Museum, Guernsey; height 120 mm.: probably early.

XLIII Comparison photograph of standard Jersey lidded half-noggin *left* and an unidentified piece with some similar characteristics (see Page 96).

XLIV Hybrid English/Guernsey Type II half-pint flagon (see Page 96).

Plates and Dishes

As far as we know virtually all plates and dishes used in the Channel Islands, certainly from the 17th to the 19th centuries, were made in England: they were identical to those made for, and used in England itself. What then, it may be asked, is the purpose of including them in a study of Channel Islands pewter? There are basically two reasons, firstly in some cases plates, by their form or by an inscription, assist in dating other Channel Islands pewter or its makers and, secondly, it is of local historical interest, since we intend to mention only those makers who also made Channel Islands flagons or measures or, if they did not make such vessels, were of Channel Islands origin.

Of the *major* makers of Channel Islands flagons and measures, so far as we have yet been able to trace, only John de St. Croix and A. Carter, with his 'accomplices' SM and CM were makers of plates.* On the other hand, Hellier Perchard and William de Jersey, both London pewterers of Channel Islands origin, were makers of plates, but as far as we ourselves know, not of flagons or measures, though Sutherland-Graeme recorded that de Jersey had, in fact, made them. It is these four only, therefore, that we shall be considering here.

With one single exception all the plates found in the Islands made by these men have had either single-reeded or plain rims, no multiple-reeded edges are known. The one exception is a five-lobed, wavy-edged plate with gadrooned rim by Hellier Perchard, inscribed 'DON DE M. IEAN DE S^te. CROIX A LA PAROISSE DE S^te. HELIER 1744' (see Plate XLV) and now kept in St. Helier Parish Church in Jersey. This piece is referred to again in Chapter 6 in connection with the life of the pewterer who bears the same name as its donor. We shall consider the wares produced by these pewterers in the order mentioned in the preceding paragraph.

Firstly, John de St. Croix: all of his dishes and plates, which are relatively scarce, both in the Islands and elsewhere, are of the single-reeded type, and range from $18\frac{1}{4}''$ down to about $8\frac{1}{4}''$ in diameter. All that we have seen bear de St. Croix's 'leopards' touch as recorded on the London touchplate and none have been found, or heard of, with the IDSX mark as found on his flagons: some of his plates and dishes also bear 'hallmarks' on the back (see Chapter 6). The fact that all are single-reeded tends to confirm our terminal date of 1765 for this pewterer, but, as will be seen in Chapter 6, the majority, if not all of his plates may well have been made 20 years or more earlier. The rim section is relatively flat, as it is in the case of most English plates and not noticeably upturned towards the reeding (see Fig. 28). Three, in particular, of de St. Croix's pieces of flatware require special mention. Firstly an $18\frac{1}{4}''$ dish, now in the Société Jersey museum, with an inscription showing that it was a 1738 replacement of an original gift of 1673 by François Le Couteur, Minister at the Parish Church of St. Martin in Jersey and secondly and

*one or two rare single-reeded plates have been found with the 'INGLES' touch noted on the 'Sark' flagon. (See page 46 *et seq.*).

XLV Wavy-edged, inscribed plate in the possession of St. Helier Parish Church, Jersey, maker Hellier Perchard. (Photo: C. Arkwright).

thirdly, a pair of $9\frac{1}{4}''$ diameter, ostensibly marriage, plates, with wriggled peacock designs incorporating the initials MИ (note reversed 'И'), and the date 1720. From everything that we know of de St. Croix, this is clearly far earlier than he could conceivably have been pewtering, and, moreover, the style and execution of the date on the plates seem to suggest a later addition. On the backs of the plates are stamped (with individual letter punches) the initials M F B, each letter surmounted by a crown. This is clearly the usual Channel Islands ownership initialling system (standing possibly for Marie Flambard) and crowned initials of this kind are frequently found on the backs of Channel Islands plates. It is difficult to reconcile the two sets of inscriptions and dating unless, perhaps, these were to commemorate an anniversary, rather than a marriage – if indeed the dates (and artistry) on these plates are not purely fictitious!

Most of de St. Croix's plates are of the ordinary flat eating or serving type, but there is a pair of good $8\frac{1}{4}''$ diameter deep alms dishes, stamped on the back 'ST. LR.', in St. Lawrence Parish Church in Jersey (see Plate XXXIII) and a very fine 18″ diameter deep dish in the possession of the author (see Plate XLVI). The general style, form and workmanship

Universitas
BIBLIOTHECA
ttaviensis

Fig. 28 Sections of rims of plates by
a. John de St. Croix.
b A. Carter.

of de St. Croix's plates suggest, in every way, a date range consistent with his Group 3 flagons, i.e. within the period 1730 to 1765, with, however, a strong bias towards the first half of that period.

Next we come to the maker, or makers, of Guernsey flagons distinguished by the coat of Arms bearing the motto 'A POSSE AD ESSE' (see Chapter 6). We have found plates and dishes with these Arms bearing also the marks A. CARTER, CM, and SM and they are not uncommon, particularly those bearing the first two marks. Again, as in the case of de St. Croix, all pieces found have had single-reeded rims (see Plate XLVII). Most have been plates of 8½″ to 9″ in diameter, especially those marked A. CARTER, but a few dishes up to 15″ in diameter have been found bearing the marks SM and CM. All the plates have an extremely close family resemblance and, in contrast to de St. Croix's pieces, the rim generally curves up perceptibly towards the reeded edge, especially in the larger sizes. (See Fig. 28). Quite frequently, also, these plates have the owners' initials (not crowned) stamped on the rim *on top of* the plate, instead of near the centre on the underside. No 'hallmarks' have been found on any of the specimens. The form and style of these plates supports our suggested date for this maker (or makers), i.e. certainly not later than 1770 and most probably generally circa 1750. However, they do appear somewhat later, and also of more utilitarian or 'commercial' character, than de St. Croix's.

Next on our list of makers is Hellier Perchard, a Guernseyman, but not, as far as we know, a maker of Channel Islands flagons and measures. Qualifying as a pewterer in London in 1709, he is the earliest of our group and, as would be expected, his plates are generally of the normal single-reeded pattern. Indeed, we have found only two not of this type – the five-lobed example in St. Helier Parish Church, already mentioned, and a 9¾″ diameter plain rim piece. This latter is interesting as it bears, not only the fairly usual label 'H. PERCHARD IN LONDON' (here *un*usually with an 'X' above), but also a hitherto unrecorded touch of the classical 'column and arch' type (see Fig. 44). Moreover, both touches are struck on the rim of the plate (on the back) and not near the centre as is usual with Perchard; the rim is relatively broad and bears, engraved on the upper surface, the device of a mitre. Generally the plate is very similar to the plain rim pieces made by William de Jersey (see Plate XLIX), which, incidentally, were also 'touched' on the rim. Remembering that Perchard took de Jersey into partnership in 1744, this is perhaps not so surprising.

Perchard's plates and dishes appear to be less common than those of 'The Carters', but not as scarce as those of de St. Croix – at any rate in the Islands. His single-reeded pieces range from 8¾″ to 16¾″ in diameter and are nearly all of normal shallow depth. The rim is usually fairly flat in the smaller sizes, but some larger dishes have been found slightly

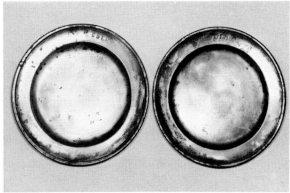

XLVII A pair of 8½″ diameter single reeded plates by A. Carter. Note owners' initials SDLM and BDLM on rim.

XLVI A fine 18″ diameter deep dish by John de St. Croix.

XLVIII A pair of 9″ diameter single reeded plates by William de Jersey.

upturned towards the reeding, similar to those of Carter. The backs are frequently stamped with Channel Islands initials in the usual form, often crowned, and also with one of two sets of 'hallmarks'.

The last of the Channel Islands plate makers that we shall deal with is William de Jersey, also a Guernseyman. He is said, by Sutherland Graeme, to have made Channel Islands flagons, but we have never seen one. Relatively few of his plates have been found in the Islands, but, in contrast to the three preceding makers, all of whom (with the exception of the two Perchard pieces already mentioned) seem to have made exclusively the single reeded type, de Jersey made plain rim types as well (see Plates XLVIII and XLIX). As he did not die until 1785, some

fifteen years after single-reeded plates are generally considered to have ceased, the incidence of plain rimmed examples is to be expected. These latter are usually around 10″ in diameter and sometimes have a lion or other device engraved on the front rim. Reeded examples have been found up to $16\frac{3}{4}$″ in diameter, again with crowned Channel Islands initials on the back, and also with 'hallmarks'. All plates and dishes so far seen have been quite shallow with relatively flat rims.

Porringers Of the whole range of 'Channel Islands' pewterers listed in Chapter 6, we have found only a single porringer, (see Plate L and LI). It is of $5\frac{3}{4}$″ diameter, with a booged side to the bowl and a single ear bearing a 'fretted' pattern of a form well-known in England up to c. 1730: stamped on the back of the ear is a mark comprising the initials AC in a chamfered rectangle, identically as found on Guernsey flagons attributed to A. Carter. We assume this piece to have been made by the same maker.

We have, however, also found in the Islands a few porringers with the touch of Jonathan Ingles of London (Cotterell 2525). These are particularly interesting in relation to certain Type I Guernsey flagons, already described, bearing a touch which we believe to be that of Jonathan's son, Thomas, and to one or two plates and an English flat-lidded flagon, all with the same touch, also found in the Islands. This suggests that there may well have been a continuing trade between the Ingles family in

L 5⅜″ diameter porringer by A.C. (Carter), (in Guille-Alles Museum, Guernsey); owner's initials MLF on top of ear.

England and the Islands from, probably, the last quarter of the 17th century. These porringers are of an entirely conventional, single-eared, booged bowl type very similar to that of AC, illustrated in Plate L.

In addition to the foregoing, we have been told by Mr. R.F. Michaelis that he has seen two porringers struck with the IDSX touch of John de St. Croix, though these pieces were obviously false. Unfortunately we have been quite unable to trace either of these pieces or to find any other examples, genuine or false! We hope that any reader who has either of these pieces or any genuine porringers by Channel Islands makers, will let us know.

As we have already stated, no other pewterware can, even indirectly, be attributed to the Channel Islands or to Island pewterers. Items such as salts, inkstands, etc. were only infrequently marked, and we have certainly not found any by known Channel Islands makers – indeed, virtually none of such items have even been found in the Islands, the local use of pewter apparently having been primarily confined to flagons, measures, 'tancars',* plates and porringers. However, there is still further scope for research, not only into new makers or new items of locally used pewterware, but also, for examples, into such questions as to whether Perchard, or indeed, de Jersey or Tysoe, ever made flagons, measures or porringers, and, on the other hand, whether Wingod, IN and other flagon makers ever made plates.

LI Detail of back of ear and touch of porringer shown in Plate L.

*a term found in 17th century inventories denoting a tankard or drinking vessel.

6 The Makers and Their Marks

Nearly all the makers included in this chapter have already been mentioned somewhere in the foregoing text. However, we made no apology for a degree of repetition in the following alphabetical list of pewterers. Neither do we apologise for venturing even further into the jungles of conjecture in this chapter than elsewhere in this book. Our deductions, from such facts as are available, and our guesses may provide collectors who are interested in the problems, with a starting point for further research or, at least, with the satisfaction of proving us wrong!

Certain of the touches are of types which are not generally associated with English makers' marks of the period. If we take the London Touch Plates as a basis for comparison, it will be noted that there are hardly any with a plain circular outline such as surround IN and IDSX, and that those which do exist are of the seventeenth century. In London, the beaded circle such as surrounds TC seems virtually to have been discontinued by, say, 1710. The ostrich feather (or palm leaf) mantling, of which traces exist in A. Carter's touch, became increasingly less used in England after 1730. Of course provincialism in art is often almost synonymous with 'old fashioned', or to put it another way, these outmoded forms of touches are indications of provincial or overseas origin. In this connection it will be noted that in the case of Jersey flagons – unlike Guernseys – none exist bearing 'London' labels, either properly written or with reversed N's.

The collection of material for this chapter has depended greatly on the generous help of many parish incumbents, curators of museums, county archivists, registrars and, of course, Mr. R.F. Michaelis. That some of the resultant theories may eventually be proved or disproved, there is no doubt, but there comes a point when one must say, 'Stop now – or go on researching for ever.' We have decided to stop!

Line drawings of *all* the touches and marks that we have found are reproduced, approximately to the actual size struck, immediately below each pewterer's heading. (except in the case of James Tysoe, of whom we ourselves have, in fact, found no Channel Islands work). In addition, photographic plates have been provided where we have felt that they would assist in the illustration of a particular touch or mark and where reasonably well-struck examples have been available: these are not, of course, intended to be actual size.

It is the chance of alphabetical listing that this list starts with a man who, as far as the authors are aware, quite possibly was never a pewterer. He is mentioned as a Jersey pewterer by non-specialist writers and given the very circumstantial dates of 1732–1785. It seems that the origin of his inclusion lies in some erroneous labelling in the Société Jersiaise Museum (long since corrected).

Bonamy, E.
(no known touch)

This mark (Cotterell No. 5530) appears struck twice on the top of the lid of apparently early Type I Guernseys. It consists of a beaded oval containing the letters TC, with two roundels above and one below. The roundels are pierced as for an axle, but are not mullets, for, instead of the usual five distinct points of a mullet or the rowel of a spur, they have small and numerous indentations like the cogs of a gear wheel within the outer circle. They may have been intended to represent mill wheels, a fairly scarce heraldic charge. We have found no family bearing such devices in their arms whose name can be associated with any pewterer known to us.

C..., T...

Fig. 29 Touch and mark of TC. (See also Plate LII(a))

The touch is accompanied by a 'London' label with reversed N's. Apart from the indication of provincialism provided by the outdated use of the beaded oval, and the fact that the touch does not appear on the London Touch Plates, it is believed that the use of the miswritten word 'London' was a fairly frequent and deliberate trade 'gimmick' of provincials in an attempt to salve their consciences or to provide an alibi if accused of fraud.

Cotterell gives no location for this maker and neither can we, though on grounds of geographical propinquity, we would guess at 'West Country'. As for date Cotterell suggests c. 1730, which may be on the late side. Carrying guesswork even further, this mark might be linked with Thomas Couch of Tywardreath, a Cornish pewterer recorded as of 1717 by H. L. Douch (Journal of the Royal Institution of Cornwall, 1969).

These flagons are rare, only four being known to the authors – three quarts and one pint. On three examples the handle is strutted, but on the other example, a quart, the handle is attached directly to the body and thus, this piece may be earlier than the other three. The quarts have twin-bud thumbpieces.

In terms of the size of his output of Type I Guernseys, A. Carter is as important in the history of the flagons of that Island as Jean de Sainte Croix is in that of Jersey flagons. Carter was undoubtedly an Englishman

Carter, A.

Fig. 30 Touches and marks of A. Carter. (See also Plate LII(b))

working in England: beyond that he remains a mystery. There is no trace of any documentary evidence as to who he was or where and when he worked. He is not recorded as a Freeman of the Worshipful Company of Pewterers, and, therefore, is unlikely to have been a Londoner.

That being the case, what we have to say about him boils down to a series of surmises and questions.

Cotterell lists him under number 825 and ascribes him to London, c. 1750. In fact, we have found no record of him in London and his almost unvariable use of a mis-written London label, with the N's reversed, on pieces bearing his full name, A. Carter, his initials AC or the initials SM, for whom we offer an explanation below, provides virtual proof that he was a provincial worker (c.f. C . . ., T . . .). Cotterell's illustrations of his touch and subsidiary marks are incomplete, in the first place because – perhaps never having seen a reasonably pristine example of the main touch – he leaves the field of the coat of arms blank, and secondly because he omits the initial mark CM.

This coat of arms, forming the main touch which is struck on single-reeded plates and on top of the lid of Type I Guernseys (normally twice) is indexed by Cotterell as the arms of Carter and Cator (sic). In Cotterell's text, a reference back to A. Carter is given under John Cater (sic) (London Y. 1725; Cott. 851) but it is surely no more than coincidence that Cator's touch is a lion's head erased resting on a crescent. In the armorial dictionaries we have consulted, we have found no Cator who bore the arms used by A. Carter. The arms as drawn for the touch consist of two lions rampant combattant with a crescent 'in chief' on a shield with a field criss-cross hatched, with rather seventeenth century palm-leaf or feather mantling. Below is the motto 'A Posse ad Esse' and above the crest, a lion's head erased. Several branches of the Carter family bore this coat with varying tinctures and mottoes. The Carters of St. Columb, Cornwall, who originated in Staffordshire, and those of Gloucestershire bore the two lions Or on a Field Azure (for which the monochrome convention is horizontal lines) and, according to a member of the family, the Cornish branch used the motto 'A Posse ad Esse'. In 1730, according to one authority but not to all, the arms on a field Sable were granted to Dr. Nicholas Carter, D.D., perpetual curate of Deal, Kent. The monochrome convention for Sable is vertical and horizontal criss-cross hatching. Diagonally criss-crossed hatching, which is a closer description of the hatching of the touch, is the convention for tinctures which, according to Woodward's Treatise on Heraldry, are so rare in British heraldry as to be 'scarcely worth enumerating'.

So, on the face of it, the pewterer Carter was using a Cornish motto below a Kentish coat of arms. And yet he was a sufficiently meticulous herald to include the crescent in chief which is of course the mark of cadency indicating a second son, or the son of a second son.

The fact that in the touches examined the lions are plain (the convention for argent) whereas in the blazon the lions are Or (which is denoted by widely spaced pin-point dots on a plain background), is not a matter of concern because the lions are slightly in relief and the dots have no doubt worn away.

We have consulted many clergymen, the county archivists of all four possible counties, at least two museum curators and the biography of Dr. Nicholas' eldest child, Elizabeth (born 1717), the blue-stocking friend of Dr. Samuel Johnson, without finding a single Carter with a first name beginning with A.

Purely as a guess on the grounds of geography – supported by the motto – we suspect that the pewterer was a Cornishman. That branch of the family had at one time south coast shipping interests which could have formed the background to his interest in Guernsey (and Jersey to which Island he probably exported plates). A John Carter is mentioned in Jersey records of 1740 as part owner of a 30-ton ship.*

It has been noted on page 48 that pieces bearing, in addition to the 'Arms' mark, the initials CM (and always having the word London properly written) generally, as far as we have seen, appear to be of somewhat better finish than AC and SM pieces, though almost all the 'Carter' pieces are of very good quality. This would seem to rule out the possibility that the wholly unidentified CM and SM were factors. The three men must have been working partners. For what it is worth a Samuel Morton is recorded as a pewterer in Penryn, Cornwall, in 1724. Mr. H.L. Douch, to whom we are indebted for this information (op. cit.), adds that had the wills been extant, other pewterers might have been traced in Penryn. The existence of a seventeenth century pewterer of the same surname suggests a family tradition.

Reference should be made to one particular 'Carter' flagon, with the SM mark. This is a quart, with Carter's usual twin bud thumbpiece, in the

*Cour de Samedi, Jersey, 1740.

possession of the Dame of Sark. It bears the owner's initials PDC standing, beyond reasonable doubt, for the Philippe de Carteret, who, as Seneschal, or, roughly, Chief Magistrate of Sark, rebuilt his house 'La Moinerie' in 1728 after it had been destroyed by fire. As Dame Sybil Hathaway told us that it was obligatory for every 'ténement' or farm property to have an approved measure for the dispensing of milk, cider etc., it seems conceivable that this flagon was made in the first years of the 1730's. Leaving aside the question of provincialism, this date may be considered confirmed in some degree by the old-fashioned mantling of Carter's touch. Furthermore, the fact that it bears the SM mark, considered in conjunction with the difference in the finish of SM or AC pieces and CM pieces, would seem to suggest that SM was an earlier partner of Carter than was CM; and, as CM pieces are relatively scarce, a partner of longer duration.

To summarise therefore, we suggest that Carter was a provincial worker, possibly in Cornwall with two working partners, just possibly called Morton, and that his working life ran from c. 1730, ending (since we have found no plain rimmed plates) c. 1770.

This is a case where we would dearly like to hear from any reader who can throw more light.

D . . ., A . . .

Fig. 31 Touch of AD.
(See also Plate LII(c))

AD within a heart, relief cast (and therefore undoubtedly a maker's touch) appears on a few Type I Guernseys. Uniquely among Guernseys, it is on the inside of the lid (see Plate LII). Examples are so rare that we know of only one half-pint and three pint flagons, described in Chapter 5. Nothing is known about this maker, but the pieces appear to be of early date. The mark does not appear in Cotterell.

de Bordeau, Jean
(no known touch)

See under du Rousseau, Pierre. Possibly a maker of some of the unmarked Group I Jerseys. On the analogy of the touch of his fellow Huguenot refugee, Pierre du Rousseau, de Bordeau, presumably would have used the touch IDB. Has any reader seen a Channel Islands piece – or indeed any pewterware – with this touch?

**de Sainte Croix, Jean
(angl. John de St. Croix)**

In the preceding chapters we have adopted the English spelling of this man's name as it is thus that he will be familiar to collectors who are acquainted with their Cotterell. In this chapter, however, which concerns personalities whose names were never anglicized, it seems appropriate to use the proper Jersey (and therefore French) spelling of the name under which the family have always been known up to and including the current Jersey Telephone Directory.

In terms of the quantity of extant work, Jean de Sainte Croix (hereafter de Ste. Croix) is by far the most important Jersey pewterer of the eight-

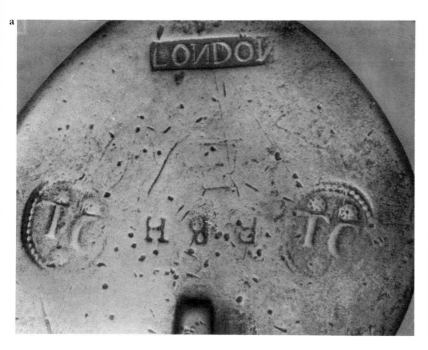

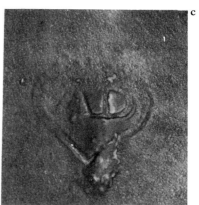

LII

Some touches and marks of:

a. TC.

b. 'Carter'.

c. AD.

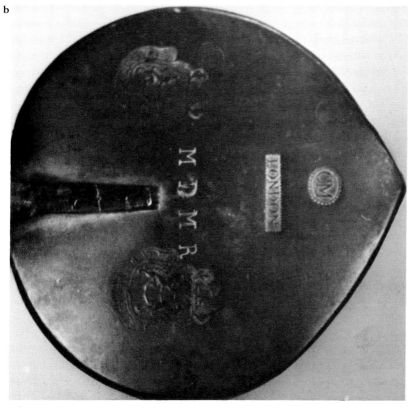

Fig. 32 Touches and marks of John de St. Croix.

eenth century. He is also the only one, apart from Pierre du Rousseau, about whom there is some documentary evidence, although this has some lamentable gaps as will be seen.

Cotterell lists him under number 1360 and illustrates most, but not all, of his marks. The touch (number 833 on the London Touch Plates) which he struck on 18th June, 1730, consists of the three leopards, or more properly lions passant gardant of Jersey and, of course, of England. The 'leopards' have, above and below, the anglicized name John de St. Croix. As a Jersey historian has pointed out, the use of these arms for commercial purposes with the name of one of the Island's oldest families in this form might well have seemed presumptuous and offensive to Jerseymen. It is likely that it was this consideration which led him to change over to the IDSX mark at a certain point in his career which will be discussed later.

This well known mark with a six pointed star above and below, all within a plain circle is illustrated in Cotterell.* So also are his subsidiary marks which include the label 'Made in London', the anglicized version of the pewterer's name in full, hallmarks IW, Britiannia, Lion's Head erased, Buckle. The buckle is sometimes replaced by a leopard's head. The Rose and Crown is also found with, above and below, 'DE ST. CROIX' and 'LONDON'. The hinge pins of flagons also sometimes bear one or other of the marks illustrated in Figure 8, Chapter 2.

The IW in the hallmarks is unidentified. The same initials appear in the hallmarks of Hellier Perchard to whom de Ste. Croix was apprenticed. Suggestions that the initials stand for Joseph Wingod are purely speculative – there is no proof whatsoever.

He does not appear to have used the Crowned X.

The combinations in which these various subsidiary marks appear

---

*Die variations have been noted with the stars differently placed in relation to the initials.

LIII Some touches and marks of John de St. Croix.
(Two photos, by C. Arkwright and author).

with the two main touches are clear cut, although not every subsidiary mark invariably appears with the appropriate main touch. Thus

(a) with the 'leopards' touch we find hallmarks and London and/or name labels. This combination appears on plates and on the deep dishes of St. Lawrence Church, Jersey, mentioned hereafter. The 'leopards' touch appears alone on rare lidded flagons which have long tongues or wedges analogous to Group 1. The 'leopards' in these cases are struck either inside, or on top of the lids.

(b) with the IDSX touch (a style of initialling used by other members of the de Ste. Croix family), we find sometimes, but not always, one or other of the hinge pin marks, but never any of the other subsidiary marks. The IDSX mark is struck on the under side of the lid of those Group 3 flagons which have shorter wedges than any other Group, though, very occasionally, it is also found on specimens with a longer than normal wedge.

There was a bye law of the Worshipful Company of Pewterers of London, of which Company Jean was a Freeman, which read 'none should strike any other mark upon ware than his own proper touch and the Rose and Crown stamp; that any man may strike his name at length between his touch and the Rose and Crown, also the word London' (11th August, 1698). The use of the IDSX touch, which does not appear on the Touch Plates, was clearly in breach of this fundamental rule. Accepted that by the middle of the century, the authority of the Worshipful Company was on the wane, they still found the energy to rule on 13th March, 1746/7, a date midway in Jean's working life, that 'all wares capable of a large touch shall be touched with a large touch with the Christian name and surname either of the maker or the vendor at full length in plain Roman letters'. The IDSX touch was hardly in conformity. Cotterell offers no explanation. The possible significance of these breaches of the rules will be discussed later.

Before leaving the subject of Jean's various marks, it is necessary to pose an unsolved problem. About twenty per cent of his IDSX flagons bear verification seals – all, with but one exception so far, of a type which, according to a regulation of Jersey's Cour d'Héritage (a branch of the Royal Court), was replaced by a new type in 1754. As will be seen in subsequent paragraphs and without prejudging the question of where he worked, evidence points to 1765 as the date of the end of Jean's active pewtering career. We have canvassed various explanations for the lack of verification marks of the post-1754 type (i.e. Seal 'B'), but without finding a convincing answer. The detail of the 1754 regulation is given on page 67. Did the Vicomte's official responsible for sealing just not bother to change the stamp he used? Surely not. Did Jean's flagons not match up to the more stringent standards laid down in 1754? Unlikely, because his capacities were always *above* the official Cabot standards and the rule was for the protection of the drinker, not the publican. Did he stop making lidded flagons and start the unlidded form? That would mean a revolutionary change of ideas about date and, by reference to the conclusion reached in Chapter 3, would have involved the use of new moulds, at least for the handles, which could have been an unacceptable expense to a successful working pewterer. Anyway, why no marked IDSX unlidded measures? Did Jean simply retire in 1754? As will be seen, it would have been an early date for retirement and only barely capable of reconciliation with the facts of 1765 to which we turn in the next paragraphs.

So much for the touches and marks. To turn to Jean's life history, there is a record of his apprenticeship to Hellier Perchard (q.v.) in London in 1722. The usual age for apprenticeship was fourteen so he must have been born in 1708 or perhaps a year or two earlier. He served his seven years' apprenticeship and was admitted to Freedom in December, 1729. He struck his touch (the 'leopards') on the London touchplate in June, 1730 and, by inference, then opened his own London workshop. Thereafter there appears to be no mention of him in London records. He was never called to the Livery and is not to be found in the London Trade Directories of the seventeen thirties and early forties. In fact, as far as London documentary sources are concerned, he disappears without trace.

In 1738, a plate (now in the Société Jersiaise Museum) bearing the 'leopards' touch was given to St. Martin's Church, Jersey. There is no reason to think that the dated inscription is not contemporary with the making of the plate. We can accept therefore that he was working in London in that year. Probably around that time a large platter and two deep alms dishes (the only known two of their type) bearing the 'leopards' were given to St. Lawrence Church, Jersey, by an unknown donor who, however, very conceivably was a member of the large St. Lawrence branch of the de Ste. Croix family. Also, three IDSX flagons, a pint and two pots, were given to the same church, perhaps by the same donor. In 1744, a gadrooned rim, lobed plate, by Hellier Perchard, was given to (and still belongs to) the Parish of St. Helier in Jersey by a Monsieur Jean de Sainte Croix. While there were several Jerseymen of the name alive at the time, it seems possible that the donor was the Jean, born *c.* 1706, who had a niece, Marie, daughter of Moise, and a grandson Moise, son of Jean, baptised in the church within a few months of one another in 1744. The fact that a de Ste. Croix donated a plate not by de Ste. Croix, the pewterer, but by his erstwhile 'master', *may* indicate that Jean, the pewterer, had by then given up making plates, due, for example, to a complete change in his business, or merely that he did not have a mould for this type of plate.

The next – and last – definite fact about Jean, the pewterer, is the issue to him of a Certificate of Origin in 1765 and published in the Bulletin of the Société Jersiaise for 1936. It reads as follows:

'Know ye that John de Ste. Croix Senr., Pewterer, Free Man of the City of London hath here shipt on Board the London Packet whereof John Lys is Master bound for the Port of London to the direction of Mr. William de Jersey in Cannon Street seven hundred pounds weight or thereabout of old pewter of the product and manufacture of Great Britain and now cast in Pigs or Ingots of eleven or twelve pounds weight a peace or thereabout, as per Oath, Given under my hand and seal at His Majesty's Castle Elizabeth, the 20th July, 1765'.

As there was only one pewterer of the name who was a Freeman of the City, there is no doubt that the Certificate was issued to our Jean and that at the time of issue, he was in Jersey. The use of the word 'Senior' requires a few lines of explanation. It was the custom in legal documents in Jersey to distinguish between members of a family bearing the same baptismal names and *in direct line of descent*, to use the appellations Senior and Junior. If Junior had a son of the same baptismal name, then on the death of Senior, the grandfather, Junior became Senior and the original grandson, Junior. Alternatively, as in the registers of baptisms which seldom, if ever, used the terms Senior and Junior, members of the same line of descent were sometimes, but not always, distinguished by the addition of the names of father, grandfather and even great grandfather. A de Ste. Croix child baptised in 1741 is described as 'fils Jean, fils Jean, fils Jean, fils Mahié'. The possibly unnecessary use of the term Senior in the Certificate is referred to later.

'Great Britain' presents no difficulty; apart from the fact that the

Islands were (and are) regarded as part of Great Britain (though not of the United Kingdom), the Islands have had from time immemorial the right of exporting their produce to England without suffering customs duty thereon. Thus the phrase is tantamount to a guarantee that the ingots did not derive from tin or pewter scarp of continental origin. As for the quantity, seven hundred pounds weight, this is equivalent to, say, two hundred and fifty Jersey pots – not excessive if it represented an accumulation of scrap from a population in excess of twenty thousand.

At first sight, an anomaly in regard to Jean's dates appeared to have arisen with the discovery of a pair of wriggled work 'marriage plates', already mentioned, bearing the leopards mark and the engraved date '1720'. However, on close examination, firstly of excellent photographs and, later, of the plates themselves, we are satisfied that the style of the digits and their engraving are not contemporary, and thus, these pieces in no way affect our chronology.

Did Jean spend all his working life in London or did he return to Jersey and thenceforward concentrate all his energies on the production of flagons bearing the IDSX mark – and if so, from what date? The fact that, in the documentary sense, he disappeared from London after 1730, does not necessarily prove that he was not in London – there were many men whose admission to Freedom is recorded and of whom thereafter there remains no written record – neither does the fact that the Jersey public records have revealed no definite trace of him, prove that he was not in Jersey.

In the first place it would be only too easy to miss a clue in the ten thousand or so unindexed pages of court records for the period 1730 to 1765. Secondly, the professions of the parties to the cases are seldom, if ever, mentioned and, in debt cases, the goods concerned are usually referred to generically as 'marchandises'. Thirdly, dealing in such an utilitarian article as pewter flagons, Jean may well have traded strictly for cash and therefore never had to sue for debt. Fourthly, even if there is somewhere a record of a Jean's house being burgled and robbed of pewterware, who is to say that the victim of the robbery was the pewterer and not one of his many cousins bearing the same name? The de Ste. Croix family in Jersey dates from 1200 A.D., if not earlier, and by the eighteenth century there were so many branches of distant cousins that it is commonplace to find bride and bridegroom with the same surname. The kind efforts of Mr. Peter Luce, Jersey lawyer, have revealed, from real estate contract records of the Royal Court, two lines of decent, both of which include Jeans with sons of the same name who, by their dates, could have been the pewterer. But equally the lower court records have produced a further Jean, son of Noe, who was summonsed for giving his schoolboy son, Jean (and therefore he was Senior at the time) a grievous kicking in the public market in 1740. The kicker *could* have been the pewterer.

Research may eventually turn up some incontrovertible record of the pewterer's presence in Jersey. Meanwhile, the preceding paragraphs have touched on certain 'indicators', none of which are individually conclusive and all of which are capable of more than one interpretation. The author and his 'coadjutors' have debated the question almost *ad nauseam*. Did Jean work in Jersey? Perhaps the most graphic way of reproducing the argument is in an abbreviated 'verbatim' fashion. The reader is the jury.

'A'. (who believes that de Ste. Croix worked in Jersey after about 1740)
The natural and obvious interpretation of the Certificate of Origin is that Jean was clearing out his workshop on retirement, having accumulated over years a quantity of broken pewterware taken in part exchange for new.

'B'. (who would be delighted if it could be proved but considers the present evidence quite inconclusive)
He could equally have been on a visit or have recently returned on retirement. And then, he could have been improving the shining hour by collecting and melting down pewter scrap for shipment to his friend, William de Jersey.

'A'. Possible. But he would have needed some sort of furnace and a ladle and moulds for the ingots.

'B'. The furnace would have presented no problem. Tin has a low melting point and moulds could have been made or obtained locally.

'A'. How could he have got away with the mark IDSX if he had been working all the time in London? And what about the regulation of 1746/7?

'B'. The Company's authority was feeble at the time. And he may have used IDSX purely as an export mark.

'A'. There is no other example that we know of where a London pewterer had a special export mark – look at the makers of Guernseys.

'B'. That is at best purely negative evidence.

'A'. Reverting to the Certificate of Origin – the unnecessary use of the word 'Senior' suggests that he was then – in 1765 – habitually known in official circles as 'Senior'. From that, it follows that he was a resident of long term.

'B'. The Lieutenant Governor's clerk who drew up the Certificate may have been over punctilious.

'A'. Why did he put IDSX – contrary to English usage – on the underside of the lids?

'B'. This is really the logical place on Channel Islands flagons as explained in detail on pages 47 and 48.

'A'. But why no IDSX plates?

'B'. Because the plates he made could just as well have been for home (i.e. English) consumption and the IDSX mark, not being English in form, might have been regarded as tantamount to Continental!

And so there is no proof either way. If he *did* return to Jersey and used, from that time, the touch IDSX on flagons only, it seems likely that his return dated from *c.* 1740. Perhaps someday someone will find irrefutable evidence one way or the other.

du Rousseau, Pierre

Fig. 33 Touch of Pierre du Rousseau.

Pierre du Rousseau whose touch is a small P:D:R within a rectangle with chamfered corners struck on the top of the lids of some Jersey Group 1 flagons, is the earliest identified Jersey pewterer, but he was not Jersey born (see page 25 et al.). There is no reason to think that he 'invented' the Jersey shape.

His work is rare. We know of only three certain examples, the pot flagon mentioned earlier in this book in St. John's Church, Jersey, which has the date 1718 inscribed on it, and another pot and a quart in the possession of the author. St. John's Church has another unmarked pot, however, which is identical to the first, and we have seen another with P:D struck on top of the lid which is almost certainly a P:D:R so badly struck that the R has not come out. No definite P:D:R work is known except these flagons (but see Appendix I).

Du Rousseau's importance is not only a matter of date. His life history, we consider, provides proof beyond any reasonable doubt that pewterware was made in Jersey, at least intermittently.

On page 54 of Volume III of the Bulletin of the Société Jersiaise in the list of those Frenchmen who, having been forced for self-preservation to adopt Roman Catholicism after the Revocation of the Edict of Nantes in 1685, escaped to Protestant Jersey and there publicly abjured the Roman faith, the following entry appears:

'1688, avril 28 Du Rousseau, Pierre, potier d'étain, de Châteauneuf, évêché de St. Malo'. This is followed by the abjuration of his wife, née Ulier. Châteauneuf is a few miles due south of St. Malo.

In the St. Helier registers of baptisms and burials the following entries appear:

Baptism. Susanne, daughter of Pierre du Rousseau of the town of Monbron (modern Montbron) in the province of Engommoy (modern Angoulême) and of Marie Ulier of the town of Guingam (Guingamp, 20 miles west of St. Brieuc), Brittany. 20 July, 1688.

Burials. The wife of Monsieur Pierre des Rousseaux (sic) was buried the 23rd day of October, 1729. Monsieur Pierre des Rousseaux was buried the 1st day of December, 1729.

The variation of spelling is unimportant and typical of the records.

From this evidence we accept that du Rousseau arrived in the Island as an already proficient pewterer and, having a family to support, probably set up as a pewterer soon after his arrival, perhaps *c.* 1690. One does not know his age at date of death, but it may be assumed that he worked until shortly before.

As a footnote, it is worth noting that the same abjuration lists mention a pewterer, Jean de Bordeau, of Châtelleraut near Poitiers, and the widow of another, Isaac Tiffeneau, of the same town. Their work, if any, remains unidentified.

This mark, in an incuse shape, has been found on only one flagon. No maker with this touch has been traced, but see Pierre du Rousseau above.

D . . ., P . . .

Fig. 34 Mark PD.(?)

Ingles, Thomas(?)

Cotterell lists Thomas Ingles under number 2527 and gives the date of his London Freedom as 25 March 1706/7. His touch is not illustrated by Cotterell in 'Old Pewter', but appears in his unpublished notes. It consists of the name (?) THO:INGLES in a curve over two rows of dots, then the date 1706 and clasped hands, the whole in scroll surround. In the examples we have seen, the first letters are only partially legible but we do not think there is much doubt about the attribution. Cotterell recorded it on a plate. We also have found it on plates and in the bottom of an English flat-lidded Queen Anne tankard now in the Channel Islands and, in combination with a large Rose and Crown, on top of the lid of a Guernsey quart in the possession of Dame Sybil Hathaway, D.B.E., Dame of Sark and on a so-far unique pint.

Fig. 35 Touch and marks of Thomas(?) Ingles.

This Sark quart bears on its lid the owner's initials E L P which most probably (see page 47) refer to Elizabeth Le Gros, a widow who, according to custom, reverted to her maiden name of Le Pelley: she became a dominant figure in Sark and died in 1726. The date range of this Sark piece is therefore 1706 to 1726, making it, with the possible exception of the TC and AD pieces, the earliest discovered Guernsey example.

It has a twin-bud thumbpiece (the pint has a twin-acorn thumbpiece) and the handle is attached to the body without a stand-off strut, a feature which is rare among Guernseys but found among the earliest Jerseys, though rare there too. It bears an unusual large London label (Plate LV), stamped in two separate syllables within a double outline: a similar label has also been noted on two other like pieces, which, however, bear no traces of the maker's touch. This Sark example bears the Rose and Fleur-de-Lys verification seals of Guernsey which were prohibited on pewterware in Guernsey until much later. Sark however could and did assert its independence.

LV Some touches and marks of Thomas Ingles.

We are reasonably satisfied, though without incontrovertible identification, that the initials Ns L Ct* struck between Tudor Roses* over the word 'GUERNESEY'* on top of the lid of Type II Guernseys (see pages 19 et seq.) stand for Nicolas le Cheminant. Apart from the fact that the le Cheminant family have apparently traditionally used this type of first-and-last-letter initialling, their family name is far better known in Guernsey than that of the le Couteurs, an essentially Jersey family, to whom Sutherland Graeme and others have suggested the initials might be ascribed.

It has already been pointed out (see Chapter 2) that the shape of these Type II flagons marks a distinct breakaway from the Guernsey tradition. However, there are very considerable differences between many specimens of this type, in weight, quality of manufacture and extent of machine finishing. These points have been examined in detail in Chapter 5 and elsewhere. On their evidence, and on that of similar Jersey pieces mentioned below, we would date them from *c.* 1780 or slightly earlier to *c.* 1830. There are however a few examples of the larger sizes, which on visual evidence, lightness and the apparent quantity of machining, could be placed substantially later, perhaps quite late in the 19th century. This is not to say that these few late pieces are reproductions in a derogatory sense but rather to suggest that to meet a continuing demand for these useful vessels, some were produced many years after the main production had ceased.

A few specimens, unquestionably of the same breed, have been found in Jersey without the initials Ns L Ct or indeed without any identification mark whatsoever. These pieces, described on pages 93 to 95, are palpably from the same moulds as some of the marked Guernseys, with, however, the neck cut down to conform to the somewhat lower Jersey capacities. Two of these examples bear the inscribed dates 1793 and 1797, a period when the international situation makes the possibility of French origin somewhat unlikely.

It is clear from these stylistic variations and the long date span that more than one maker was involved: also, the continuing use over the period of the Ns L Ct mark makes it virtually certain that this was a merchant's trademark (which had probably remained in use long after the death of its first user), rather than a maker's touch, and certainly not an owner's mark, as has been sometimes suggested.

The makers remain unidentified. At least as far as the first three decades of the period, it is improbable that they were French. In Guernsey, there was no tradition of island pewtering and there is no mention of any island pewterer in a very comprehensive island Trade Directory of 1826. This negative evidence, therefore, all points to English makers.

As for the presumed le Cheminant firm, neither the Guernsey Museums

Ns L Ct
(Le Cheminant, Nicolas)

Fig. 36 Marks of Ns L Ct.
(See also Plate LVI)

*These marks vary in size from flagon to flagon: this is *very unusual indeed* in Channel Islands marks. The example above is taken from a quart flagon.

LVI Marks of Ns L Ct.

nor the Guernsey Chamber of Commerce, which was founded in 1808, has any record of a firm bearing this name or of one using these initials. In a negative sense, this evidence could suggest that le Cheminant and his successors were Guernseymen operating in, and exporting from England. But, if so, would they have used the 'Guernesey' label? Alternatively, it is just conceivable but no more that the trade mark was originally used by a Nicolas le Cheminant who was a sea-captain-cum-merchant in the 1780's.

N..., I...

Fig. 37 Touches of IN.
(See also Plate LVII(a))

IN (see pages 41 and 42) is recorded by Cotterell under number 5815 A. His touch is IN struck in a plain or serrated circle. We are inclined to think he was a Jerseyman, working either in the Island or in England. His touch is unlike most contemporary English touches and is always placed (like IDSX) on the underside of the lid, whereas English makers of Guernseys (there are no identified English makers of Jerseys) always put their touches on top of the lids, and makers of English flagons never put their touches on the lids at all at this late date.

He does not appear to have made anything except what we have called Group II Jerseys and which we date between 1725 and 1740. Since our dating would have meant a relatively short working life for the pewterer, it may well be that he overlapped to a somewhat greater extent with Jean de Ste. Croix.

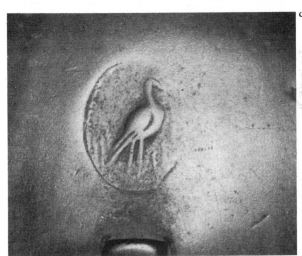

Sutherland Graeme, apparently following Cotterell (*'Pewter Down the Ages'*), named him as John le Nevew. We have no idea what evidence Cotterell had for this identification. Always on the assumption that he was a Jerseyman, we consider this interpretation of the initials most unlikely, wherever he worked. A Channel Islander called Jean le Nevew (or le Neveu) would never have omitted the 'le' in writing his initials: furthermore, the syllabic form of initialling was used almost invariably. Thus the initials would have read ILNV or, rarely, ILN. The names, Jean Noel or Néel, common enough in Jersey and, from the initialling point of view, monosyllabic, are, we consider, much more likely. It is interesting and suggestive to note that there are in Jersey two Villes ès Nouaux (Noels' Town). One of these in the First Tower/Bellozanne area is contiguous to an area traditionally inhabited by part of the de

LVII
Touches and marks of:
a. IN.
b. PSH.
c. 'Stork'.

Ste. Croix family. There are a number of instances of intermarriage between the two families.

Some IN flagons bear number 8 hinge pin mark (see Fig. 8).

PSH

Fig. 38 Touch and marks of PSH. (See also Plate LVII(b))

This touch, in a rectangle, accompanied by two Tudor roses and the label 'GUERNESEY' appears struck on the top of the lid of one Guernsey Type I pint flagon of apparently late date. There is no evidence of the identity of this maker. Purely as a guess, the initials could stand for P(ierre) Sohier, a well known name in Guernsey, Jersey and France. In fact, a Patrice Sohier is recorded as a pewterer in Alençon, Normandy *c.* 1670, some three quarters of a century, perhaps, before this single PSH flagon was made. However, we do not for a moment suggest that this piece was made in France.

'Stork'

Fig. 39 'Stork' touch. (See also Plate LVII(c))

In his article in the *Antique Collector* of May 1938, Sutherland Graeme noted this as the touch of a maker of Jerseys. We have seen one example in the Island on a pot-sized flagon, but cannot be certain whether it is the actual piece seen by Sutherland Graeme or another. The owner has no recollection of Sutherland Graeme examining it. The device (see Plate LVII) consists of a bird, probably a stork but possibly a crane or heron, facing right and standing among reeds or rushes, within an oval surround. The point of particular interest is that it is struck on top of the lid, for which reason and no other we include this piece in Group 1. It remains unidentified. Details are given in Appendix I.

Tysoe or Tisoe, James

Cotterell number 4755. His touch was a portcullis (London Touch Plates 854). He was admitted to Freedom 1733, struck his touch 1734, took Livery 1746, died 1771. He worked in Westminster. He is said by Sutherland Graeme (in the article we have quoted repeatedly) to have made Channel Islands flagons (? Guernseys). We have never seen an example.

Wingod (or Wingard), Joseph

Fig. 40 Touches and marks of Joseph Wingod.

A maker of now scarce Guernseys, Wingod is listed by Cotterell under number 5233. He was admitted to Freedom on 14th December, 1721, struck his touch (London Touch Plates 774) on 10th October, 1723, rose progressively to Master in 1767. He is recorded as having been of Tower Wharf in 1776.

His touch as drawn in 'Cotterell' shows a man giving a boy a thrashing but in his revision of Massé's '*The Pewter Collector*', Michaelis, having had the advantage of examining the plastic reproductions of the Touch Plates, describes the scene as 'a beadle leading away an offending child'. This form of touch, however, has not been found on any Channel Islands flagon: the invariable touch used on these pieces – as far as we have seen –

being a Rose and Crown in a 'classical' surround with WINGOD above and LONDON below struck twice on top of the lid together with a London label in which the two syllables are divided by a colon, the whole within a double outline.

Because of the presence of the initials I W in the hallmarks used by both Jean de Ste. Croix and Hellier Perchard, it has been suggested that there was some business arrangement between all these men. Cotterell shows no hallmarks for Wingod himself. We know of no evidence to support this association theory.

We have found Wingod Guernseys in pot, quart and pint and half-pint sizes. We know of no other types of pewterware by him.

The above completes the list of known makers – and, in the case of Ns L Ct, of presumed vendors – of Channel Islands flagons whether they worked in the Islands or in England. Jersey Group 4 (see page 45) adumbrates an unknown French maker of late Jerseys. There remain to be noted two important Channel Islanders who worked in London, but who do not appear ever to have made 'Channel Islands' pewter, that is to say flagons or measures, and also those English pewterers who appear to have had a significant export trade to the Islands of plates and perhaps other pewterware, but not Channel Islands flagons.

de Jersey, William

William de Jersey (Cotterell number 1349), son of Henri de Jersey, a Guernseyman, is quoted by Cotterell in Makers and Marks (Batsford edition 1969) page 44, as an example of an abnormal career in the Worshipful Company. He was a maker of plates, inter alia, and, according to Sutherland Graeme (but not to our knowledge), of Channel Islands

left LVIII Touches and mark of J. Wingod.

LIX Some touches and marks of William de Jersey.

Fig. 41 Touches and marks of William
de Jersey.
(See also Plate LIX)

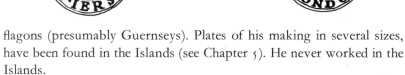

flagons (presumably Guernseys). Plates of his making in several sizes,
have been found in the Islands (see Chapter 5). He never worked in the
Islands.

He was apprenticed to Hellier Perchard (q.v.) on 25th February, 1731.
Made Free in 1738, it is reasonably assumed that he worked as a journey-
man under Perchard until 21st March, 1744. On that date, according to
the Minutes of the Court of Assistants, 'he was called in and desired to
strike his touch and to become partner with Mr. Perchard. Which was
granted. Ordered that the said Mr. Willm. de Jersey be and is called upon
the Livery of this Company and be accepted thereof and was cloathed
accordingly and paid his fine to the Renter Warden being . . . £20'.

(It is to be noted that Cotterell was wrong in saying 'Y. 1732'. Thanks
to information supplied by Mr. Michaelis, this date is amended to 1738.)

In fact, Wm. de Jersey did not strike his touch in 1744, but as a partner
of Perchard continued to make pewterware bearing Perchard's touch,
but identifiable by the hallmarks, viz. Wm de J. in a shield (which it
seems Cotterell had never seen clearly), an eagle displayed, lion's face,
lion passant.

On 19th June 1755, he sought leave again and struck his touch (London
Touch Plates 970), which is 'Party per fesse az. and gu., an eagle displayed
arg.'

This mark is found accompanied by a Rose and Crown with 'DE
JERSEY' above and 'LONDON' below on single reeded plates.
Another subsidiary mark which, as we have found it only on plain-
rimmed plates, we take to be later, is a rectangular cartouche containing
the words 'Wm. DE JERSEY' over 'IN LONDON'. This we have
always found with the Crowned X over it.

After 1744, William's career was:
        1755 fined for refusal to serve as Steward.
        1760 fined for refusal to serve as Renter Warden.
        1765 received shipment of pewter ingots from Jean de Ste. Croix
             (q.v.).
        1772 Under Warden.
        1773 Master.
        1785 died.
His shop in London was at 38, Cannon Street.

Hellier Perchard was another Guernseyman who lived and worked in London. His importance in this history stems more from the facts that he had a lifelong connection with William de Jersey and that he was Jean de Ste. Croix's 'Master' than from any pewterware he made. So far as we are aware he never made Channel Islands flagons and, although his plates are found in the Islands, he probably did not make a deliberate speciality of the Islands export trade. No doubt related in some degree of cousinship, albeit possibly remote, to the well-known Perchard silversmiths of London, he was the son of one 'Elias, merchant, Isle of Guernsey'.

He was apprenticed on 4th July 1702, to Charles Johnson (Cotterell No. 2627), of London, who was Searcher to the Company, 1698. Hellier Perchard is listed by Cotterell under No. 3611. He was admitted to the Freedom on 11th August 1709, and struck his touch on 27th August of that year. This consists of an anchor superimposed on 'G' with the date 1709 and above 'HELLARY', below 'PERCHARD': another somewhat similar touch bears the Christian name 'HELLIER'. A third touch, of a rather different type (see Fig. 42), has also been found – so far only on a single plate – but on this the first name is indecipherable. The first two of these touches are found accompanied, on his earlier pieces, by the

**Perchard, Hellier
(or Hillier or Hellary)**

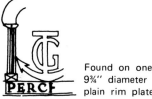

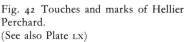
Found on one 9¾'' diameter plain rim plate.

Fig. 42 Touches and marks of Hellier Perchard.
(See also Plate LX.)

LX Some touches and marks of Hellier Perchard.

hallmarks of Jabez Harris (Cotterell 2148) – viz., Lion passant, Leopard's head crowned, Fleur-de-lys and IH – indicating an association or partnership with Harris.

Perchard was clothed in the Livery on 7th June 1714 and was Steward of the Pewterers' Company in 1719: thereafter, he was fined for not serving as Renter Warden in 1728, was Under Warden in 1738 and Master in 1740. He took William de Jersey (q.v.) as partner in 1744, presumably following the death or retirement of Jabez Harris (examples of whose plates have been found in Jersey collections). It was presumably at this time that he changed his hallmarks and thenceforth used, Swan, Globe, Lion passant and IW. It has been suggested, as in the case of de. Ste. Croix, that the IW indicates an association with Joseph Wingod, but, so far, there is not one tittle of supporting evidence.

He died in 1759.

His apprentices were:

Peter Des-amaras† (probably de Saumarez), son of Michael Des-amares, merchant, late of Guernsey – for 7 years from 17.6.1714.

James Bishop 1717–1724.

Jean de Ste. Croix 1722–1729.

William de Jersey 1731–1738.

Samuel Perchard 1737–1743.*

Simon Viveash 1748–1755

John Floyde 1741–1748.

†We know of no pewterware that can be attributed to this man. On the basis of the usual Channel Islands 'initialling' system, he would be likely to use 'PDSM' as his mark.

*Possibly a relation of Hellier Perchard but with no known C.I. pewter connection.

James Fontaine 1745–1752.

Robert Porteus 1753–Perchard's death in 1759.

John Badcock 1757 to Perchard's death when he was transferred to another Master. All these men are listed by Cotterell, except Des-amares, but their Master and their dates of apprenticeship have been supplied by Mr. Michaelis, as has all the information about Des-amares.

Turning to the exporters, the following is a list, probably not exhaustive, of English pewterers who appear to have been regular exporters, mainly of plates, to Jersey. This conclusion rests on the presence, more or less frequent, of specimens of their work in Jersey family collections which, as far as can be ascertained, date back before the time when pewter collecting as such became popular. In the case of Guernsey, since all, or almost all, of its flagons were made in England by men who, with the possible exception of Wingod, made other wares, the 'exporters' have in the main been covered in the preceding pages. In addition, no doubt most, if not all the undermentioned exporters to Jersey also sent wares to Guernsey. In one case only, Gabriel Grunwin (Cotterell 2039: London Y. 1681), have we found examples of his work in Guernsey but none in Jersey:

A. Carter (q.v.) apparently exported plates to Jersey as well as Guernsey.

Robert Dawe (Cotterell 1326), Exter, *c.* 1670–*c.* 1720.

Jonas Durand (Cotterell 1475) London, 1692–1735.

Richard Going (Cotterell 1909) Bristol, 1715–1764.*

Fasson & Sons (Cotterell 1640) London, 1784–1810.

Jabez Harris (Cotterell 2148 – see under H. Perchard) London, Y. 1694.

The 'French' names of Fasson and Durand should not be taken as indicating any special connection with the Channel Islands, although Durand is a well known name in Guernsey.

To conclude this chapter, fraught as it is with problems of detail, we cannot but succumb to the temptation of posing a general question. As the reader will have noted, as far as Guernsey Type I flagons are concerned, apart perhaps from the two shadowy characters AD and PSH, all the makers were Englishmen working in England. By contrast, none of the makers of Jerseys are recorded as being Englishmen or as having worked in England with the exception of Jean de Ste. Croix – and he, arguably, for only part of his working life. Why? Did French Huguenot refugees such as Pierre du Rousseau tend to land and stay in Jersey rather than Guernsey, simply because the former island is nearer to the Port of St. Malo, and did a tradition of local manufacture spring up in Jersey rather than Guernsey for this reason?

The answer is not clear but the contrast between the two islands in the field of pewter is evident.

*Going also appears to have exported English flagons, at least to Jersey.

7 On Collecting

In this Chapter we shall endeavour to provide information of a specific nature wherever possible, on various aspects of collecting Channel Islands pewter, to offer a few suggestions on what to collect and to give an occasional warning on possible pitfalls. Our aim is to assist not only those who may wish to specialise in Channel Islands pewter, but also those who need only to identify or purchase the odd piece.

First of all, we should perhaps give some idea of the scope of our enquiry, in particular its coverage in terms of pieces examined upon which our empirical diagnoses have been made and from which, in some cases, our theories have been developed. As regards flagons and measures, we ourselves have examined in detail, measured and photographed at least 450 pieces; similar detailed information on a further 50 or so pieces has been received from extremely reliable outside sources in the United Kingdom, Europe and the U.S.A. Rather more superficially (i.e. primarily searching for special features), we have looked at least another 100 and have received similar general information from elsewhere on perhaps a further 50. In all, therefore, a total of around 650 pieces represents the 'sample' on which our findings are based. How many more Channel Islands flagons and measures still exist we do not know: perhaps this is only a third or a quarter or even a tenth of the world total, though we have tapped so many sources that the latter seems unlikely! In any case, in relation to the size and population of the Islands it is a goodly number. Compare it for example with any English county; take Rutland (for those that remember it), the erstwhile smallest County, but nevertheless twice the area of all the Channel Islands put together. Remember, too, that the population of Jersey in the 18th century was only about 20,000 with perhaps a further 10,000 in total in Guernsey and the other Islands. Even 650 *surviving* pieces, therefore, represent a very considerable heritage: how many 'Rutland' pieces still exist? A 'silly' example, perhaps, for, as far as we know, there were no Rutland pewterers at all, but how many pieces of equal age exist that can definitely be allocated to *any* county or area outside London itself? Certainly we feel that our sample is an entirely justifiable basis for such conclusions as we have drawn, though we accept that new pieces will inevitably continue to come to light with features that may affect our theories and possibly even contradict what we believe to be our facts!

As we have previously mentioned we have prepared (Appendix I) a comparative table of statistics of Jersey lidded flagons, including what we consider to be the most significant features. Obviously it would be neither practicable nor useful to list individually every piece that we have examined and we have had to be selective. What we have done is to deal with each Group separately, as follows, in the light of the number of specimens, or different varieties of specimens found.

Group 1 – because of their comparative scarcity we have listed nearly all pieces found which we consider to be *proven* examples of this Group.

Group 2 – only representative pieces in each size have been listed because of the general uniformity of this group.

Group 3 – here again we have generally listed representative pieces in each size but have also included examples exhibiting differences in touch, wedge length, hinge pin marks, etc.

Group 4 – as in the case of Group 2, because of their general uniformity, only representative examples in each size have been listed.

In addition to the foregoing Groups we have listed separately a few examples, mainly in the smaller sizes, which, as already explained, there is some difficulty in assigning to a particular Group due to lack of identifying marks. We have, nevertheless, in most cases suggested a possible Group or Groups for these pieces and hope that this will assist readers in identifying similar unmarked pieces.

At this stage it may be useful to set down our ideas as to the comparative rarity, not only of the four Groups themselves, but also of the sizes within each Group, though excluding the two small sizes of noggin and half-noggin because *no example with a touch of any kind has been found in the former size and only two pieces in the latter*: grouping, therefore, remains a matter of personal assessment. We have of course included these sizes in our overall figures for 'All Pieces Examined'. It will be noted also in the following Table, that no assessment has been made in regard to pints and half-pints of Group 1. This is because so far we have found no absolutely proven example of these sizes in this Group. We have used a rarity system often used for coins, viz: Common (C), Scarce (Sc.), Rare (R), and Extremely Rare (ER), but it should be remembered that even the 'commonest' Jersey flagons are scarce. For example, only some ten pieces of all sizes and Groups have been offered for sale in the major London auction salerooms in the $2\frac{1}{2}$ years prior to July 1972 and seven of these were in one sale (and were not identified in the catalogue as 'Channel Islands'). Even in the Islands themselves it will certainly be a matter of weeks, and often of months before a 'new' piece appears in an antique shop or auction sale. We have decided against giving any indication of monetary values, which we have considered to be quite inapplicable to a work of this kind and which would, in any case, become out of date very quickly – possibly even before publication.

TABLE OF COMPARATIVE RARITY OF JERSEY FLAGONS

	Pot	Quart	Pint	Half-pint	Noggin	Half-noggin
Group 1 (a)	ER	ER	see preceding paragraph in regard to			
1 (b)	Sc	R	assessments for these sizes.			
Group 2	Sc	R	ER	ER		
Group 3	C	C	Sc	R		
Group 4	ER	Sc	R	R		
ALL PIECES EXAMINED	C	C	Sc	Sc	R	ER

Turning now to Guernsey flagons, we have listed in Appendix III a representative selection of Type I pieces by each of the known makers in the various sizes found and included a few pieces showing special characteristics. Similarly in regard to Type II we have included examples in each size (with a few variants) and separately we have listed some of those pieces found which, though clearly of the Type II shape, are without the normal Ns L Ct mark and are generally of Jersey capacity.

As in the case of Jersey, we append below a table of comparative rarity: again 'Common' is only relatively so and indeed Type I Guernseys by themselves are possibly slightly scarcer than the total of Jerseys, but taking into account Type II, as well, there is probably little essential difference between the two 'Islands' in the total number of extant pieces. It should be noted that very rarely is a Type I piece found without a touch and close examination suggests that any such pieces have generally merely lost their original marks through corrosion or other means: they can usually be fairly readily identified by reference to the particular characteristics of known makers or touches and have been so included in the following Table. We have not, however, included the possible hybrid pieces definitely without touches, some of which have been described in Chapter 5.

We have, on several occasions, referred to certain Jersey pieces, particularly in the smaller sizes, not readily identifiable with one of the four Groups, normally by reason of the absence of a touch. We shall now illustrate by a specific example how such pieces may sometimes be 'grouped' by reference to the essential characteristics of the known

TABLE OF COMPARATIVE RARITY OF GUERNSEY FLAGONS

TYPE I

	Maker	Pot	Quart	Pint	Half-pint	Note
	INGLES	—	ER	ER	—	— indicates no
	WINGOD	R	Sc	Sc	ER	pieces found in
	TC	—	ER	ER	—	this size
CARTER ARMS	AC	C	C	C	—	
	SM	C	C	C	—	
	CM	Sc	Sc	Sc	+	+ one possible
	PSH	—	—	ER	—	example
	AD	—	—	ER	ER	
	ALL MAKERS	Sc	C	Sc	ER	

TYPE II

	Pot	Quart	Pint	Half-pint
Ns L Ct mark	Sc	C	C	ER
No mark (gen. Jersey capacity)	ER	—	R	ER

Groups as set out in Appendix II and Chapter 2. The example is a pot 248 mm (9¾″) high to the lip, with a capacity of 2100 ccs and a wedge length of 37 mm. It has no marks other than owner's initials, no verification seal and no decoration in the form of incised lines except the usual single line at the top of the base moulding. Despite the lack of a touch this is clearly not a Group 1 piece – the wedge is too short, the handle has a strut, the shape is mature and very graceful, and the fairly usual decorative lines are lacking (this also rules out Group 4). We are left with Groups 2 and 3: the height is greater than the general run of the latter pieces but approximates to the former, and the wedge length conforms exactly to Group 2. The style, also, is right for this Group, the acorns are well defined and 'prickly' and, to cap the identification, close examination of the hinge pin reveals, beneath some corrosion, the mark of a cross (No. 8 in Fig. 8) found otherwise only on flagons of the maker IN. Despite, therefore the lack of a touch or a verification seal (found invariably so far on IN pieces), we place this flagon unhesitatingly in Group 2. This is the sort of analysis that is suggested for doubtful pieces and Appendices I and II will assist in such assessments. Similarly, Appendices III and IV will help to identify Guernseys which have lost their marks or where they are illegible.

It is perhaps appropriate at this time to issue a word of warning. Although generally there do not appear to be any counterfeit or modern copies of Channel Islands flagons circulating (though R.F.Michaelis reports de St. Croix's touch on a pair of obviously fake porringers), flagons or measures are occasionally met with that have been 'made up' or altered from their original form. For example, one sometimes finds a flagon with a lid which clearly did not originally belong to it. The simple hinge pin attachment makes it relatively easy for a good lid to be coupled with a good body, irrespective of maker, thus conceivably altering the Grouping of the piece as far as Jerseys are concerned or perhaps creating an apparently 'new' Guernsey Type. Sometimes such a practice is given away by the relative size of the lid, or by the height or some other dimension of the flagon not being in accordance with the norms as set out in our Appendices, but it is always wise in case of doubt to examine the hinge pin carefully for tampering, though of course this does not necessarily indicate a made-up piece; very occasionally hinge pins appear to have become loose or been removed or even renewed for some reason or another, but the lid still appears to be original to the body. Another 'trick' is the conversion of a flagon that has lost its lid to an unlidded measure by sawing off or otherwise removing the hinge boss. This usually leaves a tell-tale depression on top of the handle, but this has sometimes been filled in, so watch this feature and remember that most unlidded measures – certainly, as far as we can see, all those of Types (a) and (c) – have a circular top without the pinched pourer at the front of the flagon! As regards handles and their struts, always examine very carefully any flagon with the handle fixed directly to the body at the lower end – pieces like this are rare and, in our opinion, early, whether they are Jersey or Guernsey. Sometimes where handles have at some period broken away from the body, they have, without any intent to deceive, been resoldered direct to the body, though they may originally have had a strut.

The preceding paragraphs have concentrated on the lidded flagon, but to complete the picture we should give some indication of the comparative rarity that we have found in our examination of unlidded measures. As we have already pointed out these are scarcer than the lidded pieces – very much so in the larger sizes. Actually the total number of unlidded measures of all kinds that have come to light amounts only to about half of the number of even Jersey lidded flagons alone. The following table gives assessments of raity in each size for Type (a) (with the unpierced hinge boss) and Type (b) (with no hinge boss) (see Chapter 3): the total number found of each Type was approximately the same. Type (c), comprising generally pieces with unusual handle shapes), has not been included in the table as so few pieces have been found.

TABLE OF COMPARATIVE RARITY OF
CHANNEL ISLANDS UNLIDDED MEASURES

	Pot	Quart	Pint	Half-pint	Noggin	Half-Noggin
Type (a)	ER	R	Sc	R	R	R
Type (b)	—	—	R	Sc	C	Sc
BOTH TYPES	ER	R	Sc	C	C	Sc

A dash indicates that no example has been found of the particular size and Type. The term 'Common', as previously explained, is only relative. The Table illustrates the following interesting points:

(a) a fairly even spread of sizes in Type (a), except for the pot (so far a unique example)

(b) no examples at all of the pot or quart in Type (b)

(c) a strong concentration in the sizes of half-pint and noggin in Type (b) and

(d) overall, a majority of specimens of half-pint and noggin sizes, slightly less in the pint and half-noggin (actually rather fewer in the latter size), and very few in the two larger sizes.

A few general remarks on the condition and care of Channel Islands pewter may be appropriate at this point. There is no doubt that the numbers of Jersey and Guernsey flagons and measures have been very greatly reduced during the last fifty years or so. Except for those individuals or families who kept and cared for their pieces for aesthetic, historical or family reasons, there was little interest in pewter at all until comparatively recently, and it was considered of negligible value. Certainly in the last war pewter suffered greatly: the Islands were under German occupation, there were shortages of all kinds and pewter, which was generally considered to be of little account, was broken up in quantity as scrap for use by plumbers and others. Moreover, it was not only during the war years that this took place, but also both before and after: we have been told of individuals who broke up hundreds of pieces! The War probably had side effects, too, on some pieces that were treasured by their owners: to preserve them from loss or damage, they were hidden away – perhaps even buried – and, due to dampness and cold, became corroded in whole or in part. Indeed, the Islands' atmosphere is not kind to pewter; the humidity is high and the air salt-laden, so that a goodly percentage of pieces are found in an at least partially corroded condition, or with a very hard, stubborn and unattractive blackish deposit. However, those pieces that have been looked after over the years have acquired a beautiful, smooth, often slightly greenish patina.

In many cases this has been due to continual polishing, no doubt with the same wax or other polish used for the piece of furniture upon which the vessel was set as an ornament, the larger sizes of Channel Islands flagons, especially perhaps the Jersey, being most attractive for such a purpose. It is, in fact, quite rare to find, in the Islands, pieces that are bright or have been cleaned of their corrosion or patina, unless they have been through the hands of a United Kingdom or Continental dealer or collector. Most local owners, not themselves specialist collectors of pewter, believe that it is wrong to clean or treat it other than by washing, waxing, or just dusting. Indeed, those who own cleaned pieces tend to be rather shame-faced about it and to stress that *they* did not do it themselves, though, in fact, almost every cleaned piece that we have seen in a private house in the Islands has been quite well done, often years ago, and has now acquired an attractive toning.

Obviously a collector is inevitably faced with the old problem of 'to clean or not to clean' and this must be a matter of personal taste. Generally, as far as Channel Island pewter is concerned, we incline to the view that, if the piece has a fine smooth patina, even if very dark, it should be preserved in that condition. Quite apart from the aesthetic aspect, the removal of the deposit will amost certainly leave the piece in a pitted, unattractive condition, which will need harsh, hard and long work with sandpaper and wheel to remove, often then with unsatisfactory results. However, if a piece is definitely corroded and, even though not flaking, has a surface rough to the touch, and particularly if of an unattractive black colour, then, in our view, cleaning down should be carried out – though only be an expert.

We do not intend to discuss cleaning methods nor the making of repairs: these subjects have been fully treated in other works by British authors and the methods used for cleaning English pewterware are equally suitable for that of the Channel Islands. As to the methods of keeping pewter in good condition, again opinions vary, but particularly in the Islands, it must certainly be kept in a dry and preferably warm place, and it needs, like most metal, periodical 'feeding' by the application of a little oil or wax. Other than that a simple wash in warm soapy water is probably sufficient with, if desired, polishing to taste by means possibly of a suitable wadding type polish.

TO CONCLUDE, we offer, for what they are worth, a few comments on the building of a Channel Island collection. The field being relatively so limited, the collection must of necessity be specialised and somewhat difficult. As far as Jersey is concerned one might try to collect a complete set of the six lidded flagons from the pot down to the half-noggin as illustrated in Plate LXI. This of itself would be difficult enough, but to attempt a complete set of one particular Group would seem very nearly

LXI A rare set of six Jersey lidded flagons from pot to half-noggin.

LXII A very rare set of *six* unlidded measures of Type (a) (with the blind hinge boss) from pot to half-noggin.

impossible, especially as no noggins, and very few half-noggins, are known with touches. Nevertheless, it would be quite feasible to obtain a set of the four larger sizes (pot to half-pint) of Group 2 or 3 and find a reasonably matching noggin and half-noggin, which might even have been made by the same maker but not been marked. One might try and build a similar set of unlidded measures of Type (a), i.e. with the un-pierced hinge boss (see Plate LXII). Clearly the pot would be rather unlikely, but the remaining five sizes should not prove too difficult. As regards Type (b) measures, the four known sizes from pint down to half-noggin can be collected without too much difficulty (see Plate LXIII), though the half-noggin may take some time to find. Also there are so many varieties in this Type that a really well matched set might not be too easy to accumulate. Type (c), too, could possibly be collected as a set, in time (see Plate LXIV): perhaps in this case in five sizes, i.e. with the $1\frac{1}{2}$ pint in addition to the pint, half-pint, noggin and half-noggin.

Below:
LXV A set of three Guernsey flagons of
pot, quart and pint sizes by 'Carter'.

Left:
LXIII A set of four unlidded measures of Type (b) from pint to half-noggin.

Guernseys are probably simpler, if one forgets the extremely rare half-pint (and possible smaller sizes not yet definitely identified): a set of four including the half-pint is illustrated in Plate XLVI. A set of three Type I flagons of pot, quart and pint can be obtained without too much difficulty, though at a price, and even a set by the same maker, particularly the 'Carter' firm (see Plate LXV). Wingod, too, could be possible, but the other known Guernsey makers highly unlikely. Guernsey Type II, also in the sizes of pot, quart and pint, can be collected with time and application, but again the half-pint will almost certainly entail a long term search.

In addition to, or instead of the foregoing complete sets, one might concentrate on acquiring pieces of as many different makers, or as many different Groups or Types, as possible, irrespective of size. Another alternative would be to concentrate on 'hybrids' or very unusual pieces: there are indeed quite a variety of possible 'collections' even in such a specialised field. To any of these one can add, to make an effective display, a variety of plates by 'Channel Island' makers, some of which are not too difficult to come by.

Far left:
LXIV A group of four unlidded measures of Type (c) comprising one and a half pints, pint, noggin and half-noggin. (Photo: R. F. Michaelis).

Naturally a collection of any of these somewhat specialised types would be greatly improved and given added interest by the introduction of complementary pieces from outside the Channel Islands. French pieces, for example, especially those from Normandy, make most appropriate companions and provide an excellent opportunity to compare side by side, art forms which grew up in such close proximity to one another and which probably stemmed from a common source. There are other Continental pieces too, which might be introduced, especially perhaps some from Holland and Switzerland. English and Scottish pieces, also, can 'fit in' admirably – after all the metal of most of the Channel Islands pewterware was certainly English, wherever it was made. So all that remains is to wish you the usual 'good hunting' and to say don't despise a piece because it is not perfect; Channel Islands pewter is getting scarcer all the time and even a quite poor piece is better than none at all!

Left:
LXVI Part of the author's collection of Channel Islands pewter.

Foreword to Appendices

The reader who studies the Appendices which follow, will, we hope, find in them valuable indications of the probable date of flagons in his possession. We believe that the measurements given are substantially correct, although we admit that errors may have crept in occasionally, due usually to the limitations imposed by politeness on the time spent in detailed measuring.

The Appendices set out comparative statistics of Jersey flagons (Appendix I), an Identification Chart for these flagons (Appendix II), comparative statistics of Guernsey lidded flagons (Appendix III), and an Identification Chart for Guernsey flagons (Appendix IV).

These Appendices suggest certain particular points of interest: for example, in regard to Appendix I, it will be noted that there are but three 'named' makers of Jersey lidded flagons, i.e. P:D:R, IN and IDSX with two other possibles, P:D (more probably P:D:R also) and 'Stork', these latter with only one identified piece each to their credit. We have, however, postulated a period of some three quarters of a century for the production of Jersey lidded flagons and the operation of three makers only over such a long period may be considered unlikely, especially if one takes account of the appreciable number of flagons without touches in Group 1, Group 4 and in the smaller sizes generally. Whilst we believe that these three 'known' makers did not always mark their work and that they may in fact, have made at least some of the unmarked pieces, certain differences in dimensions and detailed characteristics, which will show up in the Appendices suggest that other flagon moulds were in existence at some period. Because of the high cost of such moulds, the skill required in their production and their durability, it is unlikely that any pewterer would have had more than one for a particular flagon size. It therefore seems quite possible that an additional pewterer, or pewterers, at present unknown, may have been operating, with their own moulds, particularly in the early period, say up to 1730. It is also possible that some of the moulds they used, or parts of them, were passed on to other and later pewterers: indeed IN and John de St. Croix may well have taken over the body moulds belonging to earlier makers; the quite close correlation of caliper measurements in certain cases tends to support this possibility.

To produce any worthwhile conclusions on this subject would require a great deal more detailed research. However, the general possibilities are worth bearing in mind in case pieces with hitherto unknown touches or the names of further pewterers of Jersey pieces come to light.

We have already, in the preceding Chapter, explained the broad basis on which the samples set out in Appendix I have been chosen. It will be noted that the four Groups of Jersey lidded flagons have been listed separately, in each case in descending order of size. The final section of this Appendix deals with the comparative statistics of a selection only of Jersey lidded flagons with no touch and of uncertain Grouping, for which we have nevertheless suggested what we consider to be their most likely Group, at least from the point of view of date. We hope that this will assist readers in the assessment of similar specimens of their own.

As regards the column headings in the Appendix, the height of the flagon is measured in millimetres from the base to the lip with the lid open, and the wedge length, also in millimetres, from the back edge of the lid to the front edge of the wedge. Verification Seals are dealt with in Chapter 4 and the varieties of hinge pin decoration (Nos. 1 to 10), in Chapter 2, Fig. 8. As regards 'Other Marks' these are generally owner's initials; in the case of Jersey flagons they are, unless otherwise stated, scratched, usually somewhat crudely, along the back of the handle.

The comparative statistics of Guernsey flagons (Appendix III), also provide one or two points of particular interest, notably the considerable variation in height (242 mm to 264 mm in the pot size for example), though with a very consistent wedge length. It will also be noted that the Wingod pieces are much shorter than the others in the pot and quart sizes but taller in the pint. A further point of interest is that in the pint size the 'Carter' flagons almost always seem to have the thumbpiece acorns set at a very wide angle, much wider than in the case of other Channel Islands flagons with this type of thumbpiece. Finally, we should perhaps reiterate one particular point illustrated by this Appendix and already mentioned elsewhere in the text, namely that, quite contrary to the case of Jersey flagons, there appear to be virtually no Guernsey pieces without a touch (or vendor's mark) other than those obliterated by wear or age.

As regards column headings, the comments already made in relation to Appendix I apply equally to Appendix III except that the owners' initials listed under 'Other Marks' are deeply stamped on top of the lid, unless otherwise stated. The question of hinge pin decoration does not arise in relation to Guernsey flagons – none have been found so adorned!

The representations of the touches and other marks in the Appendices are diagrammatic only: for detail purposes reference should be made to the line drawings in Chapter 6 and the photographs.

Collections of Channel Islands pewter may be seen in Jersey at the Société Jersiaise Museum in Pier Road, St. Helier and in Guernsey at the Lukis and Guille-Alles Museums in St. Peter Port.

GROUP 1 (Nos. 1 to 4 inclusive are Group 1(a), remainder Group 1(b)).

Ref. No.	Size	Height (mm.)	Touch	Wedge (mm.)	Verif. Seal	Other Marks	Decoration	Capacity (ccs)	Remarks
1	Pot	239	⦿P:D:R (See Plate LIV) on top of lid	53	None	DONNE A L'EGLISE DE ST. IEAN 1718 (stamped on lid)	2 lines at lip, 1 line each at neck and body joints, 2 lines at base.	2144	Earliest dated C.I. flagon. Thick base. Slight strut to handle. Slightly domed lid.
1A	Pot	259!	As No. 1 above	50	None	MHR on lid	2 lines at lip, reeded band at neck, 2 lines each at belly and base.	2155	Medium base with deep well under. No strut to handle. Flat lid. Note height.
2	Quart	183	As No. 1 above	41	None	EP (on handle)	2 lines at lip, 1 line at base.	1084	Thick base. No strut to handle. Slightly concave and rather pointed lid.
3	Pot	240	⦿P:D on top of lid	56	None	MPV (on handle)	1 line at base and projecting fillet around neck joint.	2154	See Page 85—touch probably incomplete striking of. P:D:R. Thick base. Strut to handle. Two concentric rings on bottom. Nearly flat lid.
4	Pot	237	'Stork' (See Plate LVII) on top of lid	48	None	MRM (on handle)	None!	2116	Unknown maker's mark. Otherwise similar to Group 3, with long wedge.
5	Pot	239	None	53	None	POUR LA PARROISSE DE ST. IAN (stamped on lid)	2 lines at lip and 2 lines at base.	2142	Virtually identical to No. 1 and probably by the same maker.
6	Pot	238	None	54	None	CBS (across handle) (engraved)	1 line at base.	2045	Note very low capacity. Thick base. No strut to handle. Slightly domed lid.
7	Pot	240	None	54	None	ILG (on handle)	2 lines at lip and 2 at base.	2095	Thick base. Strut to handle (but resoldered). Nearly flat lid.
8	Pot	250	None	56	None	MT (on lid)	2 lines at lip and 2 at base.	2101	Thick base; deep well under. Strut to handle (but resoldered). Slightly concave lid. Acorns tilted forward.
9	Pot	239	None	53	None	MM (on handle)	2 lines at lip and 2 at base.	2112	Thick base. Strut to handle (but resoldered). Slightly concave lid.
10	Pot	244	None	53	None	EMR (on handle)	2 lines at lip and 2 at base. Slight swelling around neck joint.	2136	Thick base without eversion. No strut to handle. Slightly concave lid. Acorns tilted forward.
11	Pot	239	None	52	None	MAB (on handle)	2 lines at lip and 2 at base.	2154	Thick base. No strut to handle. Body joints very noticeable. Nearly flat lid.

Ref. No.	Size	Height (mm.)	Touch	Wedge (mm.)	Verif. Seal	Other Marks	Decoration	Capacity (ccs)	Remarks
12	Pot	239	None	51	None	RLM (on handle)	None!	2125	Thick base. Strut to handle. Flat lid. Acorns tilted forward.
13	Pot	242	None	60	None	SM&EL (on handle)	2 lines at lip and 1 at base.	2108	Thick base. Slight strut to handle. Slightly concave lid.
14	Pot	240	None	54	None	ILBJ (on handle)	None!	2120	Medium base. Strut to handle. Slightly concave lid. Resembles Group 3.
15	Quart	181	None	41	None	IIM (on handle)	2 lines at lip and 2 at base.	1032	Thick base. Slight strut to handle. Flat lid.
16	Quart	180	None	40	None	IILC (on handle)	2 lines at lip and 2 at base.	1068	Thick base. No strut to handle. Flat lid.
17	Quart	184	None	41	None	None	2 lines at lip and 2 at base.	1087	Thick base. Slight strut to handle. Nearly flat lid.
18	Quart	183	None	40	None	None	2 lines at lip and 2 at base.	1070	Thick base. Slight strut to handle. Slightly concave lid.

GROUP 2

Ref. No.	Size	Height (mm.)	Touch	Wedge (mm.)	Verif. Seal	Other Marks	Decoration	Capacity (ccs)	Remarks
19	Pot	247	(See Plate LVII) Inside lid	37	'A' on left	IHC (on handle). Hinge Pin No. 8	1 line at base	2212	Normal (i.e. not thick) base. Slight strut to handle. Slightly domed lid. Well defined lower acorn cups. Well made.
20	Pot	246	As No. 19	37	'A' on left	EL (on handle) Hinge Pin No. 8	1 line at base	2145	As No. 19 with slightly longer strut to handle and almost flat lid.
21	Pot	247	As No. 19 above	37	'A' on left	PGB (on handle) Hinge Pin No. 8	1 line at base	2094	As No. 19 above, but with *very* 'prickly' acorns.
22	Pot	246	(See Plate LVII) Inside lid	36	'A' on left	SDC (on handle)	1 line at base	2179	As No. 21 above.
23	Pot	247	As No. 22	36	'A' on left	EN (on handle)	1 line at base	2130	As No. 21 above.
24	Pot	247	As No. 22 above	36	'A' on left	LBP (on handle)	1 line at base	2145	As No. 21 above.
25	Pot	247	None!	37	None	PLCN (on handle) Hinge Pin No. 8	1 line at base	2100	As No. 21 above. Despite lack of touch and Seal, adjudged to be Group 2 (see Chapter 7)
26	Quart	178	As No. 22 (See Plate LVII) Inside lid.	32	'A' on left	ELR (on handle)	1 line at base	1101	Normal (i.e. not thick) base. Strut to handle. Almost flat lid. Well defined lower acorn cups. Well made.

Ref. No.	Size	Height (mm.)	Touch	Wedge (mm.)	Verif. Seal	Other Marks	Decoration	Capacity (ccs)	Remarks
27	Quart	180	As No. 26	32	'A' on left	MLC· (on handle)	1 line at base	1100	As No. 26 above.
28	Quart	178	As No. 26	32	'A' on left	ELGL (on handle)	1 line at base	1104	As No. 26 above.
29	Pint	138	As No. 26	25	'A' on left	MDC (on handle)	1 line at base	535	As No. 26 above.
30	Half-pint	110	As No. 26	19	'A' on left	IBH (on handle)	1 line at base	257	As No. 26 above.
31	Half-noggin	68	As No. 19	12	'A' on left	MRR (on handle)	1 line at base	63	As above, but acorns close together and somewhat rudimentary.

GROUP 3

Ref. No.	Size	Height (mm.)	Touch	Wedge (mm.)	Verif. Seal	Other Marks	Decoration	Capacity (ccs)	Remarks
32	Pot	236	John de St. Croix 'Leopards' (See Plate LIII) *on top of* lid.	55	None	MAB (on handle)	One line around base. Hinge Pin No. 7 (See Fig. 8)	2085	Thick base. Strut to handle. Slightly concave lid. Round, smooth acorns. Well made.
33	Pot	239	As No. 32	55	None	ILF (on handle)	As above	2095	As above.
34	Pot	239	As No. 32	55	None	—	One line around base	2100	As above.
35	Pot	237	John de St. Croix (IDSX) (See Plate LIII) inside lid.	57	None	PPL (across handle)	One line around base	2223	Normal thickness base. Strut to handle. Flat lid of unusual shape. Not best workmanship.
36	Pot	237	As No. 35	40	None	ELM (on handle)	As above	2259	Normal thickness base. Strut to handle. Slightly domed lid. Well made.
37	Pot	241	As No. 35	39	None	ADLP (on handle)	Line around base and Hinge Pin No. 7 variant. (See Fig. 8)	2100	As above.
38	Pot	238	As No. 35	32	None	MLB (on handle)	One line around base	2136	As above.
39	Pot	241	As No. 35	32	None	—	As No. 37	2075	Normal base. Strut to handle. Slightly domed lid. Well made.
40	Pot	239	As No. 35	32	'A' on left	STS (on handle)	One line at base. Hinge Pin No. 5 (See Fig. 8)	2104	As above.
41	Pot	239	As No. 35	29	None	ABL (on handle)	As above but Hinge Pin No. 2	2195	As above.
42	Pot	239	As No. 35	29	'A' on right	ILR ⇌ SGF 1751 on handle (engraved)	One line around base	—	As above.

Ref. No.	Size	Height (mm.)	Touch	Wedge (mm.)	Verif. Seal	Other Marks	Decoration	Capacity (ccs)	Remarks
43	Pot	237	As No. 35	28	None	ST. LORAIN on handle (engraved)	One line around base. Hinge Pin No. 1 (See Fig. 8)	2146	As above.
44	Pot	242	As No. 35	28	None	DDGT (on handle)	As above but Hinge Pin No. 3	2085	As above but thick base.
45	Quart	182	John de St. Croix 'Leopards' (See Plate LIII) *inside* lid	38	None	ARN (across handle) (engraved)	One line around base	1070	Thick base with deep well under. Almost no strut to handle. Flat lid, rather pointed. Well made.
46	Quart	183	As No. 45	39	None	MGLC (Across handle) (engraved)	As above. Hinge Pin No. 7	1072	As above.
47	Quart	181	(IDSX) inside lid (See Plate LIII)	27	None	ILG (on handle)	As above, but Hinge Pin No. 6	1081	Normal base with rather deep well. Otherwise as No. 42.
48	Quart	174	As No. 47	25	None	P. ENOUF (stamped on handle)	As above but Hinge Pin No. 2A (i.e. No. 2 with 'dot' only.	1071	As No. 42.
49	Quart	183	As No. 47	25	None	MBN (on handle)	As above but Hinge Pin No. 4	1089	As above.
50	Quart	181	As No. 47	25	'A' on left	SAB (on handle)	One line around base	1075	As above.
51	Pint	145	As No. 47	22	As above	IG (on handle)	As above	524	As above but with narrow wedge.
52	Pint	143	As No. 47	24	'A' on left	MPL (on handle)	One line around base. Hinge Pin No. 7	530	As No. 42 but not best workmanship.
53	Half-pint	115	As No. 47	27	'A' on left	IG (on handle)	One line around base. Hinge Pin No. 7 (See Fig. 8)	254	Normal base. Strut to handle. Slightly domed lid. Well made. Relatively long wedge– ? early.
54	Half-pint	117	As No. 47	22	'B' on right	EIN (on handle)	One line around base	261	Normal base. Strut to handle. Very large, almost flat lid. Five flanged hinge instead of usual three. Well made.
55	Half-pint	118	As No. 47	21	'A' on right	None	One line around base. Hinge Pin No. 10	261	Similar to above but deep well (8 mm) under base and lid not quite as large.
56	Half-noggin	70	As No. 47	17	As above	None	One line around base	64	Normal base. Strut to handle. Well made.

Ref. No.	Size	Height (mm.)	Touch	Wedge (mm.)	Verif. Seal	Other Marks	Decoration	Capacity (ccs)	Remarks
GROUP 4									
57	Pot	251	None	38	'B' on right	None	Two incised lines at lip, one at base of neck, two just below belly, one at base. Hinge Pin No. 8 (with 'dahlia' boss)	2120	Fairly thick base, outward curved. Strut to handle. Slightly domed lid. 'Prickly' acorns. Well made with substantial machine work.
58	Quart	179	None	32	'C' on right	None	As above	1055	As above.
59	Quart	182	None	32	'B' on right	None	As above	1070	As above.
60	Quart	180	None	34	None	None	As above	1067	As above.
61	Pint	140	None	20	As above	None	As above but large undecorated boss on hinge pin.	515	As above.
62	Pint	140	None	19	As above	None	Similar but no boss on hinge pin	518	As above.
63	Half-pint	115	None	20	'B' on right	I L R (on handle)	As No. 57 but 2 lines at base of neck and small undecorated hinge pin boss	260	As above.
64	Half-pint	115	None	20	'B' on right	None	As above but lines at lip wider apart	261	As above.

COMPARATIVE STATISTICS OF CERTAIN JERSEY LIDDED FLAGONS WITH NO TOUCH AND OF UNCERTAIN GROUPING

Ref. No.	Size	Height (mm.)	Wedge (mm.)	Verif. Seal	Marks	Decoration	Capacity (ccs.)	Remarks	Conjectural Grouping
65	Pot	242	45	'B' on right	SLB (across handle)	None but variant of Hinge Pin No. 7	2150	Thick base. No strut to handle. Slightly concave lid. Acorns tilted forward.	These two flagons have very similar measurements. The base, lid and general appearance, and the hinge pin on No. 65, could place them in Group 1 or early in Group 3, say c. 1730.
66	Pot	238	45	None	EBD I (on handle)	None	2145	Thick base. Slight strut to handle. Flat lid.	
67	Quart	178	33	None	LBT Z (on handle)	One line at base and four light lines below belly. Hinge Pin similar to No. 8	1082	Normal base. Strut to handle. Slightly domed lid. 'Prickly' acorns. Well made.	The characteristics of these two flagons and their dimensions are similar to Group 2. The Hinge Pin device on No. 67 is also very close to that found on Group 2.
68	Quart	178	33	'A' on left	IAM (on handle)	One line at base	1072	As above.	

Ref. No.	Size	Height (mm.)	Wedge (mm.)	Verif. Seal	Marks	Decoration	Capacity (ccs.)	Remarks	Conjectural Grouping
69	Half-pint	117	26	None	None	Two lines at lip	266	Thick base. Slight strut to handle. Acorns tilted forward. Pronounced body joints.	The general characteristics of this piece—base, lid, acorns, etc.—suggest Group 1 period.
70	Half-pint	108	20	(A) on left	LF (on handle)	One line at base. Hinge Pin No 8	254	Normal base. Strut to handle. Flat lid. Well made.	The dimensions and general characteristics of these two pieces are similar to Group 2. Note also Hinge. Pin No. 8 on No. 70 and Seal 'A' on left side of both pieces— also indications of Group 2.
71	Half-pint	110	19	As above	EGC (on handle)	One line at base	260	As above but lid slightly domed.	
72	Noggin	92	12	'A' on right	MPS (on handle)	One line at base	131	Normal base. Strut to handle. Almost flat lid. Not best workmanship.	Possibly Group 3, perhaps of early period.
73	Noggin	97	12	'B' on right	None	Two lines at lip, two just above base, one at base	128	Slim shape. Normal base. Strut to handle Slightly domed lid. Well defined acorns. Large undecorated Hinge Pin boss.	General characteristics of these two pieces suggest possibility of Group 4.
74	Noggin	94	12	As above	None	As above with one additional line above belly	129	As above	
75	Noggin	95	12	As above	IDN (on handle)	Two lines at lip, two at neck and one at base	130	Slim shape. Normal base. Strut to handle. Slightly domed lid. 'Prickly' acorns. Well made.	This piece, as the two preceding, may also be Group 4, but but could perhaps be earlier.
76	Half-noggin	72	12	None	None	None	67	Thick base. Nearly flat lid. Slight strut to handle. Solid construction.	Note high capacity of 'Guernsey' standard. These two pieces have some of the characteristics and appearance of Group 1 and we tentatively assign them to that Group.
77	Half-noggin	73	12	Rose & Fleur-de-lys. (Guernsey)	MVD (on top of lid)	Two lines at lip	68¾	Similar to above but with acorns tilted forward.	
78	Half-noggin	67	12	'A' on right	None	None	63	Normal base. No strut to handle. Slightly domed lid. Well made.	Possibly Group 2, despite Seal being on right side of lip, or early Group 3.
79	Half-noggin	66	13	As above	None	One line at base	63	As above but slight strut.	Probably Group 3— perhaps of early period.
80	Half noggin	66	13	As above	None	As above	63	As above.	

Conjectural Date	Group	Touch	Maker	Wedge Length	Base Rim	Handle and Thumbpiece	Decoration
1695 to 1725	I(a) I(b)	[P:D:R] [P:D] } (See Plate LIV) 'Stork' (See Plate LVII) all on top of lid None	Pierre du Rousseau Probably as above Unknown Unknown. Possibly several, including du Rousseau	Generally 51 mm to 56 mm in pot size – 40/41 mm in quart.	Thick, i.e. 5 mm to 6 mm in pot size – 4/5 mm in quart.	Handle thick and strong. No strut or only rudimentary. Round and 'realistic' acorns.	Usually two lines at the lip and one or two at the base, rarely plain.
1725 to 1740	2	[I N] or [I N] inside lid (See Plate LVII)	Unknown. Cotterell (5815A) gives John le Nevew, but unlikely (see text). Possibly Jean Noel or Neel.	36/37 mm in pot size – 32 mm in quart.	Thinner, i.e. usually about 3 mm in pot size – slightly less in quart.	Handle fairly thick and strong with strut at foot. Round, well formed acorns, often 'prickly'.	Usually only a single line at top of base mould. Hinge Pin No. 8 (see Fig. 8) found on some examples.
1730 to 1765	3	Coat of Arms with three leopards & JOHN DE ST CROIX on top of, or inside lid, or [IDSX] inside lid (See Plate LVIII)	John (or Jean) de St(e). Croix. (Cotterell 1360)	55 mm on the 'Leopard' pots; others generally 28 mm to 32 mm, but occasionally longer. 'Leopard' quarts 40 mm, others 25/27 mm	'Leopard' pieces are thick as Group 1. Others about the same as Group 2, but sometimes a little thicker.	Handles similar to Group 2, and with strut at foot. Acorns vary – some similar to Group 2, others more oval than round and with quite smooth surfaces.	Usually only a single line at top of base mould, but a variety of decorated hinge pins (see Fig. 8)
1790 to 1830	4	None	Unknown Possibly French (see text).	38 mm in pot size – 32 mm to 34 mm in quart – 19/20 mm in pint.	Thicker than Groups 2 and 3 and out-curved (see Fig. 12)	Handle as Group 3. Acorns very well formed with 'prickly' cups – casting line often visible.	Usually two lines at lip, one at bottom of neck, two just above base and one at base eversion. Large decorated hinge pin boss on many examples. (Fig. 8, No. 9)

1780 to 1830   WE ATTRIBUTE TO THIS DATE RANGE CERTAIN SPECIMENS WHICH APPEAR TO BE OF GUERNSEY TYPE II, THOUGH OF JERSEY CAPACITY AND WITHOUT THE NORMAL 'GUERNESEY' AND OTHER MARKS, AND WHICH SEEM TO HAVE BEEN USED IN JERSEY. THESE ARE DEALT WITH IN APPENDIX IV.

Verif. Seal	Other Characteristics
None	Solid and heavy construction. Belly sometimes appears not so rounded as in the case of the other Groups. Lid often slightly concave or flat, rather than domed. So far specifically identified only in pot and quart sizes. This is a chronological, rather than a maker's, Group.
Seal 'A' always on left side of lip (looking from handle forwards)	5 mm to 6 mm taller than other Groups in the pot size. Very graceful and extremely well made and finished. Lid usually almost flat, but sometimes slightly domed. NOTE – an occasional flagon without a touch can be attributed to this Group (see Chapter 7).
80% None: remainder Seal 'A' on left *or* right side of lip. Rare example with Seal 'B'	Largest Jersey Group comprising about half of all lidded flagons found. More varied in shape and detail characteristics than other Groups. Usually well made but occasional inferior examples found. Lid almost invariably slightly domed. NOTE – Two touches ('Leopards' and IDSX) with different characteristics – the former somewhat resembling Group 1. Some unmarked flagons, especially in the smaller sizes, may belong to this Group.
Seal 'B' on most examples. Seal 'C' or none on others.	So far a relatively small Group of well made pieces, mainly of quart size, showing evidence of considerable machine finishing and usually in a very good to immaculate state of preservation. Contrary to the almost universal practice in other Groups, almost no examples have been found with owner's initials. Lid slightly domed. NOTE – Characteristic 'dahlia' hinge pin boss found so far on all pots and quarts but not on smaller sizes.

COMPARATIVE STATISTICS OF GUERNSEY LIDDED FLAGONS

Ref No.	Size	Height (mm.)	Touch on top of lid except where stated	Wedge (mm.)	Veri Seal	Other Marks	Decoration	Capacity (ccs.)	Remarks
1	Pot Type I	242	Joseph Wingod (See Plate LVIII)	38	None	⟨LON:DON⟩ and I N T (stamped on lid)	Three reeded bands around neck and similar at belly. Incised lines at skirt.	2202	Strut to handle. Flat lid. Twin acorn thumbpiece. Well made.
2	Pot Type I	253	Carter 'Arms' struck twice & AC (See Plate LII)	37	None	LONDON and I D L M (stamped on lid)	As above	2170	As above.
3	Pot Type I	251	Carter 'Arms' struck twice & SM (See Plate LII)	39	None	LONDON (stamped on lid)	As above	2190	As above.
4	Pot Type I	260	As above	37	None	LONDON and I D G (stamped on lid)	Three reeded bands around neck and 7 lines around belly. Lines around skirt.	2200	As above
5	Pot Type I	254	Carter 'Arms' struck twice & GM (See Plate LII)	37	None	LONDON and D M Q (stamped on lid)	As above but 9 lines around belly.	2116	As above.
6	Pot Type I	264	None but may have been obliterated	36	None	J B K (stamped on lid)	Three reeded bands around neck only. Lines around skirt.	2212	As above. May be made by maker of No. 4.
7	Pot Type II	243	Ns L Ct (See Plate LVI) Probably a vendor's mark.	30	Rose & Fleur-de-lys	GUERNSEY with two Tudor Roses and N B (stamped on lid)	None	2196	Generally Jersey shape but with skirt (rudimentary). Slightly domed lid. 'Prickly' acorns. Poor workmanship.
8	Quart Type I	200	Thomas(?) Ingles (See Plate LV)	30	Rose & Fleur-de-lys	LONDON and crowned rose stamped on lid. (See Plate LV)	Three reeded bands around neck and similar around belly. Incised lines around skirt.	1090	Strut to handle. Flat lid. Twin bud thumbpiece. Fairly well made.
9	Quart Type I	198	TC struck twice (See Plate LII)	31	None	LONDON and P B H (stamped on lid)	Three reeded bands around neck and similar around belly. Lines around skirt.	1080	Strut to handle. Flat lid. Twin bud thumbpiece. Not best workmanship.
10	Quart Type I	184	Joseph Wingod (See Plate LVIII)	32	None	⟨LON:DON⟩ and O M (stamped on lid)	As above	1070	Strut to handle. Flat lid. Twin acorn thumbpiece. Well made.
11	Quart Type I	199	Carter 'Arms' struck twice & AC (See Plate LII)	26	None	LONDON and I R B (stamped on lid)	As above	1140	Strut to handle. Flat lid. Twin bud thumbpiece. Well made.
12	Quart Type I	195	Carter 'Arms' struck twice & SM (See Plate LII)	28	None	LONDON and T C H (stamped on lid)	As above	1130	As above.

Ref. No.	Size	Height (mm.)	Touch on top of lid except where stated	Wedge (mm.)	Veri. Seal	Other Marks	Decoration	Capacity (ccs.)	Remarks
13	Quart Type I	199	Carter 'Arms' struck twice & ⊙CM⊙ (See Plate LII)	28	None	LONDON and ICB (stamped on lid)	Three reeded bands around neck. Nine lines around belly. Lines around skirt.	1122	As above with slightly 'prickly' buds.
14	Quart Type II	189	Ns L Ct (See Plate LVI) Probably a vendor's mark.	31	None	GUERNESEY with two Tudor Roses and PLPT (stamped on lid)	One incised line around skirt.	1085	Generally Jersey shape but with skirt (well proportioned). Slightly domed lid. 'Prickly' acorns. Well made.
15	Quart Type II	188	As above	34	Rose & Fleur-de-lys	As above but IBH	As above	1075	As above.
16	Pint Type I	160	⟨AD⟩ (See Plate LII) Relief cast inside lid	30	None	PM (stamped on lid)	Two lines each side of raised body joint at neck and belly. One line at lip and one at base of neck.	608	No strut to handle. Flat lid. Twin acorn thumbpiece. Wedge resembles Jersey type. Not best workmanship.
17	Pint Type I	161	⟨TC⟩ (See Plate LII) Struck twice	28	None	LONDON and MLM (stamped on lid)	Three reeded bands around neck and similar at belly. Lines around skirt.	592	Strut to handle. Flat lid. Twin acorn thumbpiece. Not best workmanship.
18	Pint Type I	162	Joseph Wingod (See Plate LVIII)	25	None	⟨LON:DON⟩ and TN (stamped on lid)	As above	590	Strut to handle. Flat lid. Twin acorn thumbpiece. Well made.
19	Pint Type I	150	Carter 'Arms' struck twice & ⟨AC⟩ (See Plate LII)	31	None	LONDON and MBH (stamped on lid)	As above	595	As above but acorns set at wide angle.
20	Pint Type I	142	As above	31	Jersey Seal 'B'	MT (stamped on lid)	As above	523	As above but NOTE—low 'Jersey' capacity.
21	Pint Type I	150	Carter 'Arms' struck twice & ⟨SM⟩ (See Plate LII)	34	None	LONDON and IDMP (stamped on lid)	Three reeded bands around neck and similar at belly. Lines around skirt.	565	Strut to handle. thumbpiece with acorns at wide angle. Flat lid. Well made.
22	Pint Type I	150	Carter 'Arms' struck twice & ⊙CM⊙ (See Plate LII)	31	None	LONDON and PMS (stamped on lid)	Three reeded bands around neck and 7 lines around belly. Lines around skirt.	555	As above.
23	Pint Type I	157	PSH (See Plate LII)	44	None	GUERNESEY two Tudor Roses and EDLM (stamped on lid)	Three reeded bands around neck and 4 lines at belly. Lines around skirt.	582	Slight strut to handle. Flat lid. Twin acorn thumb-piece. Well made.

Ref No.	Size	Height (mm.)	Touch on top of lid except where stated	Wedge (mm.)	Veri. Seal	Other Marks	Decoration	Capacity (ccs.)	Remarks
24	Pint Type II	152	Ns L Ct (See Plate LVI) Probably a vendor's mark.	20	Rose & Fleur-de-lys	GUERNESEY with two Tudor Roses and R D L M (stamped on lid)	None	550	Generally Jersey shape but with skirt (well proportioned). Slightly domed lid. 'Prickly' acorns. Well made.
25	Half-pint Type I	126	Joseph Wingod (See Plate LVIII)	30	None	LON:DON and R N T (stamped on lid)	Four lines simulating reeded bands at neck and belly.	271	Generally Guernsey characteristics but no skirt. Flat lid. Twin acorn thumb-piece. Multiple flanged hinge. Well made.
26	Half-pint Type I	126	As No. 25	25	Rose & Fleur-de-lys (twice)	LON:DON (stamped on lid)	Three slightly raised lines (close together) at neck and belly.	270	As above.
27	Half-pint Type II	121	Ns L Ct (See Plate LVI) Probably a vendor's mark.	22	Rose & Fleur-de-lys	GUERNESEY (stamped on lid) and two Tudor Roses.	None	275	Generally Jersey shape but with skirt (well proportioned). Slightly domed lid. 'Prickly' acorns. Well made.

COMPARATIVE STATISTICS OF LIDDED FLAGONS OF GUERNSEY TYPE II SHAPE, BUT UNMARKED AND GENERALLY OF JERSEY CAPACITY

Ref No.	Size	Height (mm.)	Touch on top of lid except where stated	Wedge (mm.)	Veri. Seal	Other Marks	Decoration	Capacity (ccs.)	Remarks
28	Pot	247	None	38	None	I V P scratched on handle	None	2157	Generally of Jersey shape but with skirt. Slightly domed lid. 'Prickly' acorns. Well made.
29	Pint	149	None	23	None	C C B 1797 engraved on belly and C C B 1793 scratched on bottom.	None	518	As above.
30	Half-pint	115	None	24	None	As above	None	260	As above.

Ref No.	Size	Height (mm.)	Touch on top of lid except where stated	Wedge (mm.)	Veri. Seal	Other Marks	Decoration	Capacity (ccs.)	Remarks

LATE AND IMPORTANT DISCOVERIES GUERNSEY TYPE I LIDDED FLAGONS

Ref No.	Size	Height (mm.)	Touch on top of lid except where stated	Wedge (mm.)	Veri. Seal	Other Marks	Decoration	Capacity (ccs.)	Remarks
	Pint	160	Thomas(?) Ingles (See Plate LV)	30	None	LONDON and RMD (stamped on lid)	Reeded bands around neck and belly. Lines around shirt.	595	No strut to handle. Flat lid. Wide twin acorn thumbpiece. Not best work. SO FAR UNIQUE.
	Half-pint	129	AD (See Plate LII) Relief cast *inside* lid.	22	None	BMQ (stamped on lid).	Incised lines at lip. Two pairs incised lines at neck and belly simulating reeded bands. One line around neck.	274	No strut to handle. Flat lid. Wide twin acorn thumbpiece. No pinched spout (? Shape altered). SO FAR UNIQUE.

Conjectural Date	Type	Maker	Touch	Other Marks	Thumbpiece and Handle	Decoration
	I	Thomas(?) Ingles	See Plate LV	Crowned Rose and 'LONDON' (See Plate LV) (Note – large unusual, 'broken' 'LONDON'.)	Twin-bud thumbpiece. Handle fixed direct to body. (Note – two possible examples have a small strut.)	Three reeded bands around neck and similar around belly.
1710 to 1730	I	Unknown	[AD] Relief cast inside lid (See Plate LII)	None	Twin acorn thumbpiece. Handle fixed direct to body.	Raised body joint between two pairs of incised lines at neck and belly. Lines at lip and base of neck.
	I	Unknown	[TC] Struck twice. (See Plate LII)	[LONDON] (Note – reversed 'И's.)	Quarts have twin-bud thumbpiece, pint twin-acorns. One piece has handle fixed direct to body, others have strut.	Three reeded bands around neck and similar around belly.
1723 to 1770	I	Joseph Wingod (Cott. 5233)	See Plate LVIII	[LON:DON] (See Plate LVIII)	All sizes have twin-acorn thumbpiece. Handles have strut at foot.	Three reeded bands around neck and similar around belly.
1730 to 1770		A. Carter (Cott. 825)	'Arms' (See Plate LII) with [AC] or [SM] or [CM] or	[LONDON] or [LONDON] (reversed 'И's.) (See Plate LII)	Pots and pints have twin-acorn thumbpiece, quarts have twin-bud. Handles have strut at foot.	Generally three reeded bands around neck and also around belly, but sometimes incised lines around belly instead of bands.
c. 1780	I	Unknown	[FSH] between two Tudor roses (See Plate LVII)	[GUERNESEY] (See Plate LVII)	Twin-acorn thumbpiece. Handle with strut.	Three reeded bands around neck, four lines around belly.
1780 to 1830 or later	II	Unknown	[Ns L Ct] between two Tudor roses (See Plate LVI) ?Vendor's mark? (See Chapter 6)	[GUERNESEY] (See Plate LVI)	Twin acorn thumbpiece with Jersey type wedge. Handle with strut.	Normally none, except one line at skirt on some examples. A very occasional piece has lines elsewhere.
		Unknown	None	None	As above	As above

Verif. Seal	Other Characteristics
Rose and Fleur-de-lys on 'Sark' flagon only. See p. 47	Rare. Only two certain and two possible examples found; one pint and three quarts. Flat lid.
None	Rare. Only four known examples, one half-pint and three pints. Flat lid. Wedge somewhat resembles the Jersey shape. High capacity. Not best workmanship.
None	Rare. Only four examples found (three quarts and one pint). Flat lid. Not best workmanship.
None	Scarce. Found in sizes of pot, quart, pint and rare half-pints with differences in detail (See Chapter 5). Flat lid. Good workmanship.
None	The commonest of the Guernsey Type I makers. Found in sizes of pot, quart and pint – usually well made. Flat lid. Detail differences between the three 'initials'. (See text). One possible half-pint noted.
None	Rare. Only one definite example, a pint, has been found and another similar body, but the lid missing. Flat lid. Well made.
Often Rose and Fleur-de-lys.	Found in sizes of pot, quart, pint and half-pint. General shape like Jersey Group 3, but with skirt. Considerable variation in quality and detail. Slightly domed lid.
None	As above, but conform to Jersey capacity standard and generally found in Jersey.

On pages 84 and 85, we have dealt briefly with two very unusual and interesting baluster measures, which appear to have certain Channel Island affinities. The purpose of this note is to examine these pieces in more detail and, in particular, to endeavour to assess more closely their relevance to Channel Islands pewter, their origin and their date. Certain information already given in the text is repeated here, both to avoid continual reference back and also so that this Appendix may form a complete entity in itself.

The first of the two measures, illustrated in Plate XXVIII(a), is a 'quart' – actually it has a capacity of 1082 cubic centimetres. In comparison, the English and Channel Islands standards are as follows – Old English Wine 947 ccs., Old English Ale 1112 ccs., Imperial 1136 ccs., Jersey 1024 ccs., and Guernsey 1064 ccs. Clearly, therefore, this aspect of the piece favours a Guernsey attribution.

The measure is 199 mm in height to the lip and has a heart (or leaf)-shaped lid, very nearly of standard Channel Islands XVIIIth century shape, (but possibly very slightly rounder), and quite unlike the usual circular lid found on English measures. The lid is quite flat, except for a very slight turn-down at the pointed front end, and so resembles that of a Guernsey Type I flagon rather than the slightly domed form of lid of Guernsey Type II pieces and of most Jerseys. The top of the flagon under the lid is now quite circular, but there are faint signs that the lip under the point of the lid might originally have been very slightly 'pinched' to facilitate pouring. This feature is found, in quite pronounced form, on all Channel Islands, and many French, flagons, though not on English balusters, which always have circular tops.

The wedge, 27 mm long, is some 14 mm wide where it joins the thumbpiece, tapering to about 6 mm at the front and sloping down fairly steeply from thumbpiece to lid: it is thus of a form very similar to that of the normal Guernsey wedge (and an occasional Jersey). The thumbpiece is a type of twin-bud – not at all like the English form of bud, but again very reminiscent of that found on many Guernsey quarts (any time from 1706 onwards, as far as our present researches go). The latter, however, usually has a quite plain, smooth surface (with, very rarely, a faint trace of 'prickles'), whereas the present specimen has a somewhat rudimentary surface design (see Plate XXVIII(b)).

Whilst discussing the lid and thumbpiece, it is convenient to compare them with French pieces as well as with English. The lid is indeed similar to some French types, though not as 'pointed' at the front as the most usual French types, and the thumbpiece, too, is of somewhat similar shape to the French 'bourgeons' – indeed the design on the surface seems faintly to resemble the form of decoration on that French thumbpiece. The wedge, again, is not unlike some of the French types, particularly, perhaps, those of Normandy.

To conclude our examination of the lid, we note that it has the initials M G R stamped thereon with individual punches. Clearly these are owner's initials and this particular form of owner's initialling is virtually unknown in England. On the other hand, it is the almost universal custom on Guernsey flagons (though rarely on Jerseys, which usually have initials scratched on the handle): similar stamped initials are occasionally found on Normandy pichets also. If they indeed refer to a Guernsey family, as we believe, then they could, for example, stand for Marie Gerard (see Pages 42 and 43 re the Channel Island system of initialling).

Turning now to the body, we see, at first glance, what appears to be an English baluster, but, on closer examination, we note that there is no collar around the top, or, rather more accurately, only a slightly angled projection. True, some of the very early English balusters were collarless, but this piece is definitely of more sophisticated form and manufacture than those pieces. Moreover, the body has a series of incised lines, comprising one at the lip, two about $\frac{3}{4}''$ below the lip at the bottom of the angled projection, two at the lower end of the neck where the body begins to swell out, two about 1'' from the bottom and two just at the top of the splayed base rim. Lines such as these are quite untypical of the earliest English balusters (which are nearest to this general shape), though they are found on later examples of generally more 'bulbous' form and with a fully developed collar. Despite these detail differences the body shape is certainly far more like that of an English baluster than of anything else that we know: it is quite unlike the main Channel Islands shapes* and equally, as far as we know, there are no generally found French types with a shape resembling this at all – certainly not in North West France, which would be the most likely area.

One very interesting feature of this piece is that the seaming is vertical, (i.e. it has been cast in two halves, split vertically), instead of following the universal practice (we believe) of horizontal seaming found in British and Channel Islands pewter. However, Charles Boucaud in 'Les Pichets d'Étain' records that early (i.e. pre-1650) French measures were cast vertically and we believe that this happened elsewhere on the Continent, for example in Holland.

The handle is strap-like and very similar in shape to that of an English baluster (and of some French pichets) and, being affixed directly to the body at the lower end, and having no out-turned terminal, would normally be regarded as 'early', say before 1650. It has a pronounced 'step' just below the hinge, not generally found on English pieces, but very common on Channel Island flagons, (perhaps intended to act as a stop and prevent damage to the thumbpiece and hinge, when the lid was opened). The inside of the handle is quite perceptibly concave, a feature we have not found on any ordinary English, Channel Island or French piece.

We should now endeavour to assess the likely origin of this piece, i.e. where it was used and where made, and its probable date. As to origin, we need examine only England, the Channel Islands and France – no other area is even remotely likely. It is perhaps convenient to consider first where the piece is most likely to have been used. England seems unlikely – except for the general shape, there are virtually no features of this piece that are in the least reminiscent of XVIIth or XVIIIth century

*but see later comments in regard to an occasional special piece of apparently Channel Islands provenance.

English hollowware and it is difficult to imagine a piece like this being sold (and used) in England in the light of the strict regulations in force and the very conservative nature of the industry (and its customers). Similarly France, too, seems very unlikely: although the lid, thumbpiece and handle could be French, and also the owner's initials, body shapes of this kind are found nowhere in France that we know of. This leaves only the Channel Islands and, in view of the lid shape, the initials thereon, the wedge, thumbpiece and handle, and the fact that the piece was actually found in Guernsey, we would definitely place this as a piece made for use in the Channel Islands, and specifically in Guernsey. True, the body shape is unconventional, but there are a few rare half-pint flagons by Joseph Wingod, c. 1725 (see Plate XXXV), undoubtedly attributable to Guernsey, and some other unidentified pieces (e.g. Plates XXXVI and XXXVIII) also certainly of Channel Islands provenance and of early date, which have not entirely dissimilar forms.

As to where this piece was made, we have two, or perhaps three, alternatives, viz., England, The Channel Islands or, just possibly France. The latter is considered very unlikely, despite the method of casting with vertical seams, as no valid reason can be seen for a French pewterer making a single piece, or a very few pieces, of generally English shape and in English metal for export to the Channel Islands. England, however, is very possible, even probable – indeed one would almost say 'certain' were it not for the very unusual vertical casting system, which seems never to have been used in the United Kingdom. On the other hand, an English pewterer exporting to the Islands (and especially to Guernsey, as we know they did) might have experimented with this method, or made the piece, or pieces, to special order for a particular Guernsey client.

Turning now to the Channel Islands themselves, we believe that Jersey can be discounted immediately: any Channel Islands' characteristics of this measure are basically of Guernsey form and it is inconceivable that such a piece would have been made in Jersey specifically for Guernsey use (this point is discussed on Page 51 in relation to Type II Guernsey flagons). As regards Guernsey itself, we have found no tradition, nor indeed even the slightest indication, of any pewter manufacture in the Island, though this is merely negative evidence. Theoretically one might adumbrate a French pewterer – for example a Huguenot refugee – settling in the Island, (where English baluster measures may well have been in use, as well as French pichets), and producing a new design based on the types with which the inhabitants were familiar, but varied by his own previous experience and training, particularly as to the method of casting. One can neither prove nor disprove this: all that one can say is that the piece is very well made, clearly by an experienced pewterer, and that, if it *was* made in the Island, it is hard to understand why more pieces have not come to light and why, apparently, its production did not stimulate further manufacture in the Island. That it did not, we can feel fairly sure, as, with a very few just possible exceptions, all Type I Guernsey flagons were almost certainly made by English pewterers operating in England.

On balance, whilst others may hold different views, it is the writer's opinion that the most likely place of manufacture of this measure is England.

As to when the piece was made, we are again in some difficulty – as with origin there is conflicting evidence. The general form of the piece and the shape and fixing of the handle appear XVIIth century rather than XVIIIth: moreover, the vertical system of casting (of which we know only of Continental examples) appears to have been superseded by horizontal seaming about 1650. On the other hand, the 'feel' of this piece, its general sophistication and its very excellent manufacture and present condition suggest a somewhat later date – perhaps early XVIIIth century. However, if this is a Guernsey piece, as we feel convinced, how does it relate in time to the typical Guernsey pieces of standard form? The earliest Guernsey maker that we know of is Thomas(?) Ingles, who qualified in 1706 and might, therefore, have manufactured Guernseys any time thereafter, especially as there is evidence to suggest that his father, Jonathan, (also a London pewterer), had been exporting other items of pewterware to the Islands: certainly we believe that Thomas was producing 'standard' Type I Guernseys by at least 1725 (see Pages 46–47). One might take the view that this baluster was an immediate forerunner of the Type I Guernsey pattern (especially in view of its capacity, thumbpiece and other features already mentioned), and, if this were so, a date prior to 1725 would be appropriate – perhaps even prior to 1706, when Thomas Ingles qualified. Taking all the foregoing points into consideration, we would be inclined to set the most probable date range of this piece as being between 1690 and 1720, inclining perhaps towards the later date rather than the earlier.

The second of the two balusters we are examining (see Plate XXVII) is a pint of 568 ccs. (i.e. in the Guernsey or Imperial(!) range). It is 152 mm. high to the lip and the lid, in contrast to the preceding example, is quite round except for a small 'point' at the front (though there is no 'pinched' pouring spout beneath, the lip of the measure being quite circular). The lid is quite flat and the wedge 30 mm long, is of the tapering and downward sloping form noted on the preceding measure. The thumbpiece is a twin-acorn, a form unknown in English pewter, but found on the great majority of Channel Islands, and many French, pieces. The acorns are somewhat rudimentary and fairly widely spaced, just like those on most Guernsey Type I pints (see Plate IX(b)). On top of the lid are stamped the initials I D G, in typical Guernsey form, which could, if of Guernsey provenance, stand for Jean de Garis, an old Guernsey family from whose possession a quantity of authenticated Guernsey pewter is known. The comments already made in regard to the lid, wedge and thumb-piece of the preceding piece apply equally to this one and we must consider these features to relate to Guernsey, rather than Jersey, England, or France.

The body of this piece is very closely similar indeed to that of the preceding piece, as a comparison of Plates XXVIII(a) and XXVII will show, even the number and position of the incised lines being identical. Both pieces, too, have a pronounced 'ridge' inside the flagon near the lip, coinciding with the second set of external incised lines, and, as in the case of the first piece, clear signs of vertical casting can be seen.

The handle shape is straplike and also, as in the case of the other piece, fixed directly to the body at the lower end. It does not, however, have the slight step (acting as a rest for the thumbpiece when the lid is open) found just below the hinge on the other, and the inner surface is only slightly concave end. It does not, however, have the slight step (acting as a rest for the thumbpiece when the lid is open) found just below the hinge on the other, and the inner surface is only slightly concave in the lower section, whereas the first piece is decidedly concave throughout its whole length.

As to where this piece was used, we see no reason to depart from the view taken in regard to the preceding piece – namely Guernsey – even though, in this case, the measure is now in England and we have knowledge of its previous provenance. In relation to where it was made and when, the arguments set out previously would appear generally to apply here too, though there are in fact, some indications suggesting that this piece may be slightly earlier, for example the general 'feel' and condition. Indeed, before the discovery of the former piece, the owner had been inclined to date this measure around 1650. However, in the light of our conclusions in regard to the possible date of that piece (i.e. 1690–1720 and probably nearer the latter), we would perhaps place this piece around 1700 or just a little later, on the assumption that it, too, was either an early experimental piece or one specially produced for a Channel Islands family and made, most probably in England, but just possibly in Guernsey itself.

We hope that the publication of this detailed note will bring to light other similar examples – perhaps even one with an identifiable touch – and that it will be possible to be more precise as to the place and date of manufacture. However, of one thing we are certain – *these must be regarded as Guernsey pieces* and probably the earliest yet found.

Acorns, twin The most usual form of thumbpiece on C.I. flagons.

Buds, twin A type of thumbpiece found on some Guernsey lidded flagons of quart size only. Not the same as English 'buds': more like elongated pips.

Cabot The basic Jersey Capacity Standard (see Chapter 4). Not represented in flagon sizes.

Engraved A term used in this work to indicate a somewhat wider and deeper decorative line on a flagon or measure than the incised line.

Flagon A lidded vessel from which liquids could be dispensed into drinking vessels such as tankards or tavern mugs. Also used in Jersey and sometimes in Guernsey as measures of approved capacity. Sometimes used to hold Communion wine.

Hinge Boss A semi-circular raised section at the top of the handle which, in lidded flagons, is voided to accommodate the moving flange of the lid hinge and is pierced to hold the hinge pin. Occurs on some unlidded measures solid and unpierced.

Hinge Pin Boss The raised end – decorated or not – of some hinge pins.

Incised A term applied to the thin, shallow decorative lines often found around flagons or measures.

Measure Although lidded flagons were sometimes used as measures, the term is used primarily of unlidded 'Jerseys'.

Noggin (Jersey-French 'Nodgin'). A measure of capacity (see Chapter 4). 'Half-noggin' (Jersey-French 'demi-nodgin') also occurs.

Ovolo A convex, quarter round moulding.

Pot The Jersey or Guernsey equivalent of two quarts: the largest size of C.I. flagon (see Chapter 4). Pronounced 'Po'.

Quarto Old Guernsey name for the noggin size. 'Demi-quarto' also occurs.

States of Guernsey The 'Parliament' of the Island of Guernsey.

States of Jersey The 'Parliament' of the Island of Jersey.

Strut A short section of metal often interposed between the lower end of the handle and the body of a flagon or measure. An 'identification characteristic'.

Tongue See 'Wedge'.

Verification Seal A seal stamped on flagons and unlidded measures to indicate 'Government approved capacity'.

Wedge Sometimes referred to as 'Tongue'. A rectangular section of varying length, cast integrally with the thumbpiece and central hinge ring of lidded flagons. An important 'identification characteristic'.

Well The cavity beneath a flagon or measure.

Specialist Sources on Pewter

BELLONCLE, MICHEL *Les Étains*. Librairie Gründ, Paris, 1968.

BOUCAUD, CHARLES *Les Pichets d'Étain*. Paris, 1958. Out of print.

COTTERELL, HOWARD H. *Old Pewter, Its Makers and Marks*. Batsford, London, 1969. *Pewter Down the Ages*. London, 1922. Out of print.

DOUCH, H. L., M. A. Cornish Pewterers, in *The Journal of the Royal Institution of Cornwall, 1969.'*

HOMER, DR. R.F., B.SC., PH.D. *Research into the Capacities of Baluster Measures*. Transactions of The Pewter Society, June 1960 and April 1961.

MASSE, H.J.L.J. *The Pewter Collector*. Revised by R.F. Michaelis, Barrie & Jenkins, London, 1971. *Chats on Old Pewter*. Revised edition by R.F. Michaelis, Ernest Benn, London, 1949.

MICHAELIS, R.F. *Antique Pewter of the British Isles*. G. Bell & Son, London, 1955. New edition by Dover Publications, New York, 1971. *British Pewter*. Ward Lock & Co. Ltd., London 1969. *A Short History of the Worshipful Company of Pewterers and a catalogue of pewterware in its possession*. Privately published, London, 1968. Unpublished Notes.

PEAL, C.A. *British Pewter and Britannia Metal for Pleasure and Investment*. John Gifford Ltd., London, 1971.

SUTHERLAND, GRAEME, CAPTAIN A.V., F.S.A., A.R.I.B.A. *Pewter of the Channel Islands*, in 'The Antique Collector', London, May 1938.

ULYETT, KENNETH *Pewter Collecting for Amateurs*. Frederick Muller Ltd., London, 1967.

VERSTER, A.J.G. *Old European Pewter*. Thames & Hudson. Out of print.

VICTORIA & ALBERT MUSEUM *British Pewter*. H.M.S.O., London, 1960.

WYLIE, W. GILL *Pewter, Measure for Measure*. U.S.A., 1952.

General and Historical Sources

Bulletins of the Société Jersiaise St. Helier, Jersey, 1875 –

Transactions of the Société Guernsiaise St. Peter Port, Guernsey, 1882 –

Registers of Baptisms, Marriages and Burials. States of Jersey and Island Parishes.

CHEVALIER, JEAN *Journal, 1643–1651*. Published by the Société Jersiaise in 9 vols. up to 1914.

EWEN, A. H. AND DE CARTERET, A.R. *The Fief of Sark*. Guernsey Press Co. Ltd., Guernsey, 1969.

FALLE, PHILIPPE *An Account of Jersey, 1694*.

LEMPRIÈRE, RAOUL *Portrait of the Channel Islands*. Robert Hale, London, 1970.

STEVENS, J., F.S.A. *Old Jersey Houses*. Jersey, 1966.

ANSTED AND LATHAM *The Channel Islands*. Revised edition 1893. Published by W.H. Allen & Co. Ltd.

Official Correspondence on the Law relating to Weights and Measures. Published in Jersey by J. Bigwood 1914.

This list would be incomplete without a sincere expression of thanks to many correspondents, clergy, curators and librarians of museums, county archivists and innocent, private recipients of our letters who have given up their time to search books and records in an effort to find answers to our abstruse questions.

Index